AF352468

NORTH/SOUTH: THE GREAT EUROPEAN DIVIDE

North/South

The Great European Divide

RICARDO J. QUINONES

UNIVERSITY OF TORONTO PRESS
Toronto Buffalo London

ISBN 978-1-4875-0005-4

∞ Printed on acid-free, 100% post-consumer recycled paper
with vegetable-based inks.

Library and Archives Canada Cataloguing in Publication

Quinones, Ricardo J., author
North/South : the great European divide / Ricardo J. Quinones.

Includes bibliographical references and index.
ISBN 978-1-4875-0005-4 (cloth)

1. Europe, Northern – Civilization.   2. Europe, Southern – Civilization.
3. Europe, Northern – Intellectual life.   4. Europe, Southern – Intellectual
life.   5. Reformation – Europe.   6. Europe, Northern – Relations – Europe,
Southern.   7. Europe, Southern – Relations – Europe, Northern.   I. Title.

DL30.Q83 2016   948'.04   C2016-901010-4

This book has been published with the assistance of the Charles and Joan
Alberto Italian Studies Institute.

University of Toronto Press acknowledges the financial assistance to its
publishing program of the Canada Council for the Arts and the Ontario Arts
Council, an agency of the Government of Ontario.

Contents

Preface

The division of European society and culture along a North/South axis – the argument of this book – is the most decisive and far-reaching event of the second half of the second millennium. To advance this argument in so slender a volume as this requires a broad sweep and an even broader purpose: it draws on the decline of nations and the nature of decline itself; it calls into service the various wings of Protestantism and the recurrence in later days and under different names of that revealing debate between Luther and Erasmus; it looks to the various failures of the Southern forces, the mystifying depths and causes of psychological and material regression, and to the Catholic rebuttal, resulting in the stalemate that would stabilize the geographic division of Europe (but not the growth of difference between the two) for approximately the next four centuries.

Given these complexities of motivation and response, this study will present critical concepts, *Christian liberty*, *scepticism*, *tolerance*, and *time*, as means for understanding how these momentous changes occurred and solidified. These concepts were transforming and transformative, and enjoyed extension and duration – geographic acceptance as well as historical length of life. They all fulfilled functions as persuasive bodies of thought that opened pathways to the future. They bring us face to face with the questions and the rewards these concepts present, the ways they are transformed into secular notions, the ways they are taken over by Protestant societies, the ways they wobble and become unsteady witnesses, even nemeses that threaten the very bases of the Protestantism that brought them forth. Each one is presented in its historical nature, as well as through a study of its own character and the tensions it produced. They represent the untold dramas this story contains.

Of the three periods where the North/South dichotomy can be addressed, the early modern, the industrial era, and the post-modern deindustrialized late twentieth century, this study directs its attention almost exclusively to the first – the one where the North/South division emerges as distinct from its immediate past but also where sufficient liberalization was attained to enable the new industrial era to come forward with its new means and machines.

This book draws near to but can offer only a glimpse of the great industrial revolution, to which it is related and with which it is continuous but different. *North/South* is of another age, with its own intellectual tools and perspectives. It does not address the mechanics and machines, the social instruments and issues, the mass movements and new class divisions between management and labor, the transformed landscapes of the industrial North and the recollected gardens of the South, and especially the vastly expanded global scope of what was to come. But it does address, where relevant, the strong similarities in argument, and this is not unexpected, because the pre-industrial developments and persuasions provided the intellectual firepower for the still future times of industry and capitalism.

This brings us once again to a major question that this slender volume pursues, one that Eric Hobsbawm sees enunciated by Marx and other social scientists, namely the need to confront "the nature and the mechanisms of the transition from pre-capitalist to a capitalist society and its specific modes of operation and ties of future development" (*The Age of Capital* 263). This remains the essential quest and argument of *North/South* – to provide the cultural tools and language with all their different characterizations for that great movement from the preindustrial early modern to the very dawn of the mechanical world that has come to dominate the centuries preceding our own. The works of modern social scientists and economic historians such as Max Weber and David Landes will frequent these pages, providing valuable insights and support (including disagreement) as they propose the great links joining the ideas (and the means) of pre-industrial Europe with the Enlightenment and the beginning of industrialization.

These very similarities of principle and procedure – necessary points of reference for this book – will require another basic alteration, one affecting chronology. Sven Beckert, in his *Empire of Cotton: A Global History* (2014), borrows a term employed in another context, the "great divergence,"[1] to characterize the ever-widening gap between the expansive North and the lagging South and pegs it as commencing in the eighteenth century (xiv). Industrialization has thus obscured what it has been one purpose of this study to expose, and that is the origins of the Great Divide under different conditions and with different means in the sixteenth century. Without discounting the prolific expansion that industrialization, colonization, and capital contributed to a continuing northern pre-eminence, there was already a remarkable split between the North and the South in Europe prior to the eighteenth century; its participants, its resources, its consequences are the subject of this work. This is not an account of the Great Divide *versus* the Great Divergence--they are not two trains heading for a collision, but rather different means of locomotion, moving in the same direction, with the one setting the path where the other will lay its tracks.

Advisories and some housekeeping

It is from a valuable range and admixture of monographs, essays, and documents that one is able to piece together into a workable whole the persons, places, and issues that comprise the matter of the Great Divide. Obviously this should be regarded as a work of humanistic synthesis rather than one of archival research. It does not pretend to offer all that is known on so massive a subject, nor to fill in detailed background material of dates and events, nor to include subordinate but important characters who provide connecting links between historically separate major figures. But it does catch at and retrieve the interests aroused in the early sixteenth century that persist through later eras, the broad lines of conflict and resolution, always relying on major figures, rightly called "high points," choosing to examine their works in all their full and comprehensive complexities, their eloquent and passionate formulations. It is preferable to follow the rich profusion of outstanding arguments found there rather than pile up a multiplicity of names and characters, with no definitive appeal. These high points all clarify and contribute to the ascendancy of the North and would extend into the late twentieth century before encountering a revival of protest and a degree of alteration in the renewed values of the once forgotten South.

Structurally the book does not adhere to a strict chronology, but with arabesques loops back on a topic in different (chiefly national) contexts. This is because concepts will have different roles in different cycles and among different national traditions. Allowances must be made for returns and revivals. To underline the larger significance of some concepts their more modern developments will be pursued. In an appendix, this study gathers into a single mosaic the ways Shakespeare's English interests extend their shadows over the continent as well. To record one of the many changes this study underwent in its own evolution, the subtitle at its origins was simply "The Great Divide," and later "The great Modern divide," and finally "the great European divide," because it was in and through Europe in that time of change, the early sixteenth century, that the foundation stones of the later constructions were laid. Retaining the more generalized "North/South" designation meant that one could avoid euphemisms – thus avoiding the dilemma of finding a counter-phrase to "advanced," or to "progressive." In contrast to the globalism of the industrial colonial age, the changes that did take place in the earlier moments, as in the later periods, occurred astonishingly enough within a small region of central to northwest Europe.

At first glance, given its make-up and scope, this argument might appear to be different from my two preceding volumes – *Dualisms: The Agons of the Modern World* (U of Toronto P, 2007) and *Erasmus and Voltaire: Why They Still Matter* (U of Toronto P, 2010). But as I engaged more fully with the materials of this volume I began to see that if not quite a trilogy – however appealing a "Toronto trilogy" might sound – the three together did represent a series of related interests. They all begin with issues in transit from the early sixteenth century to the Enlightenment. They all search out the great continuum extending between the two. They all are comparative in approach, in fact representing at their fullest the idea of a predominant dualism. And still harkening back to the volume of that name, in practice they depend upon Coleridge's great critical principle of recognition, the recognition of genuine similarities within the more obvious dissimilarities (*Dualisms* 198–202).

Acknowledgments

Here I am pleased to indicate and to thank the friends and colleagues who have reviewed, refereed, or simply read this work: Ms Joel Black, the late Linda Brooks, David Michael Hertz, Erika Rummel, Paul Barolsky, Eva Brann, Jay Martin, and Robin Vaccarino. My two assistants, Anthony Desoto and Marlon Batiller, saved me from panic over the complexities of my computer, and above all, my dear wife, Roberta L. Johnson, made some immensely practical and critical suggestions that brought the book much closer to its realization.

I am very grateful to Hiram Chodosh, president of Claremont McKenna College, for his generous subsidy in aid of publication of this volume.

NORTH/SOUTH

Chapter One

Groundwork

Freedom of religion is the very first commitment of civil society ... All the other freedoms that civil society requires such as freedom of speech, of the press, of association ... are extrapolations from that one central freedom, the freedom of religion.

Robert Bellah[1]

This is a story of dramatic changes in the intellectual and political topography of Europe. The onset, expansion, and consolidation of a Europe divided between countries of the North and those of the South is the most striking, widespread, and enduring development of the modern world. This division in matters of religion, government, economics, technology, military power, and intellectual life was devastating to the conventional understanding and values of the Middle Ages; both Catholic Christianity and Islam were stymied and held to a virtual standstill by the new developments. The new North/South polarity represented a radical redirection from the cartography of the Middle Ages, once controlled by East/West conflicts, in which Spain and southern and central European areas were besieged for centuries by successive Byzantine, Arab, and Ottoman forces. Among the last meaningful observances of the East/West divisions before their revival in the second half of the twentieth century was a pacific but crucial one, occurring in 1493 when Pope Alexander VI, in a series of bulls, assigned Portugal's sphere of influence to the East and that of Spain to the West, a decision confirmed by both maritime parties at the treaty of Tordesillas in 1494 (a treaty that would naturally offer no restraint for later Protestant seafaring entrepreneurs). But not until the sea battle of Lepanto (1571), which became so much a part of the Spanish mythos of the *reconquista*, did Spain wrest control of the western

Mediterranean from the Turks. However celebrated the victory, it left the Ottoman Empire and Spain in a stalemate, with which neither was too displeased as each had other concerns.

The markers of change and renewal are plentiful from 1550 forward. The South that once controlled the Mediterranean basin and beyond (under the Romans) endured, in the time period here under study, a long period of relegation to secondary status. In contrast, in our time, the genius of the original conception of the European Union lay in its intention to bridge the gap between northern and southern Europe, particularly when the current geo-political dynamic seemed to be moving towards a restored East-West dichotomy. But the would-be resurgent powers of the South have temporarily regressed, recalling and even exacerbating the long historical division between northern Europe and its neighbours to the South. This becomes, then, a contemporary story but one revealing the continuing presence of the past, of avatars once thought subdued but showing a viral resistance to elimination.

The very engines and arguments that powered the emergence of the European North provided the pattern for other parts of the world, where the same divide was repeated. So remarkably persistent in its diffusion has the North/South dichotomy become, that when the topic is googled it results in thousands of hits for essay entries. Many of these are preposterously irrelevant; some are of only local importance (North and South Tahoe); and others, even more numerous, relate to military and strategic questions, even if of artificially created importance (North and South Koreas and Viet Nams). Then there are those addressing questions raised by the many parties representing Africa of the North – the Mediterranean littoral – and sub-Saharan Africa.

Tribal and racial differences aggravate these divisions. Politics and religion are factors in separations within individual nations. Some countries traditionally considered part of the North have known sharp internal divisions along North/South lines; examples include the United States, France – whose south once comprised a separate nation, Occitanie – and the United Kingdom, where England, perhaps paradoxically, plays the southern role to Scotland, a region with which it is conjoined in the north. Similarly, some countries of the South can show a fairly strong Northern aspect (Italy and Mexico among the most prominent). Mme de Staël, in her *De l'Allemagne*, has offered stunning comparisons between the north and the south of Germany and between Germany and France.[2] Some regions of the South have known historical surges only to fall back again, as witnessed by the fortunes of such decidedly Southern representatives as Greece, Italy, Portugal, and Spain. Ireland is obviously a very special case; it could be considered Southern, if not geographically then in its mentality and history. Its history testifies that more is involved here than questions of simple geographic location.[3]

We know that there is a north beyond "the North" and a south beyond "the South." If our object were purely geographic, to borrow George Orwell's quip, the only true Northeners would be the Esquimaux. Our purpose is to understand the *géographie symbolique*, that is, the geographic designation in all its political meaning. Of course the North and the South have their physical centres of response, their centres of gravity – be they Rome, Seville, Geneva, or London, Holland, Berlin, centres for inclusion or exclusion, for acceptance or opposition. They are psychic centres for the organization of beliefs and practices. They can provide banners under which armies march, and goals towards which faiths are plied. The geographic designations we employ involve ways of life, philosophical and religious bearings, attitudes towards others. These preliminary comments treating historical frameworks and manifestations will be developed with greater precision and clarification in the chapters that follow.

For the moment two examples, one taken from England and the other from France, show two different ways of working to establish or to challenge the North/South division and provide snappy or fetching titles for these approaches. J.H. Hexter has called them "splitters and lumpers"; Le Roy Ladurie has referred to their separate callings as "parachutists and truffle hunters"; and one can invoke Isaiah Berlin's "hedgehog and fox" dualism. The one is empiricist, dealing with details, looking for exceptions to grandiose schemes and principles, while the other seems to focus on wider perspectives, and the sweeping grandeur of generalities. The broad topics chosen seem to call for broad principles of understanding. Their divergences are both historical, that is, growing out of their engagements with historical change, and inherent, lodged in temperament, and their own psychic needs.[4]

With respect to England, detailed studies are available, primarily of geographic and economic import. Indications of such scholarly interests are present in the collection of essays, *Geographies of England: The North-South Debate Imagined and Real* (eds. Baker and Billinge, 2004), where the very title suggests the warring tensions between the scrupulous empiricism, even positivism, typical of many of the essays, and the acceptance of a serious and singular North/South divide. For instance, even when discussing the industrialized North of England and its apparent triumph, other factors are introduced to discount its mastery: the predominance of London as the financial and cultural centre, and the persistence of core-periphery grids which undercut any singular divide. Most of the essays involve substantial questioning of the very possibility of a North/South divide. What are the boundaries, where does the South leave off and the North begin? There is no consensus among the authors, but rather an acknowledgment of "pockets" of varying strengths and finally the recourse to the bromide that such generalized divisions are "imagined," mere constructs, and not "real." The North/South divide does strike a chord, however, in discussions of the postmodern deindustrialized age when the service and financial interests of the South rose to pre-eminence, contrasting sharply with the economic decline, the empty warehouses, and deserted factories of the North. The North/South divide is a direct expression of this transformation (Martin 30). One could add however that the North/South divide found equally clear expression in the transformations of other times and places.

Geographically, given its large physical mass, France was predisposed to a North/South divide, the famous Saint Malo-Geneva line (Le Roy Ladurie). Whatever the nuances and refinements, France has long been influenced by a separation between the North and the South. This is a physical as well as historical separation. Le Roy Ladurie can on occasion be dismissive of the contemporary usefulness of this cartographic separation, finding it somewhat outdated, particularly when the contrast is based upon a rich North versus a poor South (a somewhat limited testing ground; Ladurie 123).

Nevertheless, geography, politics, and finally religion contributed to the acceptance of a great French divide. In France the region of the South, the Sud, the Midi, while subdued and subservient in time to the North, has been strangely persistent in its customs, in its language and accent, and its literary expression.[5]

The centralizing tendency of the French monarchical powers, one of the consequences of the Edict of Nantes and the newly secured kingship of Henri IV, concentrated power in the capital city of Paris. The strife and migrations of the sixteenth century moved the Huguenots from their positions in the North to settlements in the South. As Le Roy Ladurie concludes in his essay, *"Nord-Sud,"* whatever the variables might be (brought about by geography and other elements), the South is *autre* and France is consequently *duelle* (double, or divided). While there is a tendency in English thought to adhere to an earnest empiricism that borders on scepticism, the sense of "the other" in French cultural thought avoids scepticism because there is always a "true" France in accordance with which that which is not so identified will always be the "other." This makes for an awkwardness in promoting toleration, as the acceptance of the "other" always derives from a superior position, that of the upholder of the true France.

One of the tests of the validity of a theme is its penetration of the vernacular. The varied associations with the North/South divide globally have surfaced in many unexpected aspects of life. Linguistically, the division has generated its own tidbits: *el Norte* in general use implies having struck it rich; more specifically, from Mexico (or Guatemala) it alludes to a hazardous journey to seek freedom and fortune in the colossus to the North. It is also used to indicate "a sum greater than," as in "a bonus just north of $10,000," while to have "gone south" means the total collapse of an enterprise. In baseball, a left-handed pitcher is a southpaw. While this term was originally employed when the layout of the playing field had the left-handed pitcher throwing from the south side, eventually southpaws became notorious for an unruly wildness, even personal eccentricities. In American football, independent of the layout of the stadium, sports broadcasters find it convenient to mark the advancement of the ball along a grid that identifies the desired direction as "North." East-West play does not measure up and fails to move the ball towards a "new" first down, and is a sign of futility. More in the line of cultural oddities, it is clear that syntactically, the word "North" will always precede "South." We never say South/North, as that would transpose the driving force.[6] To provide a similar instance, the theme of Cain and Abel is always registered in that order (there is one exception, Baudelaire's poem *"Abel et Cain"*). Syntactically, priority suggests actual pre-eminence.

In a wider context the South as sinister is marked by suppositions that an ill-wind blows from the South, a "sinister" event for plants and animals; and Europeans have been taught to fear the *föhn* or the sirocco. Jean Bodin in his *Six Books of the Republic*, drawing his contrasting differences between North and South, is sure that "Northerners feel languid when the south wind blows" (147).

The use of the North/South dichotomy as a descriptor has its roots in a body of issues that began in Europe in a particularly contentious time. This North/South image was later extended throughout a surprisingly large part of the world. Its origins were sectarian and religious, but the division was perceived even more strongly in secular times. While the concept was one that originated within nations, it became more generally transnational, and has endured well into the nineteenth century and beyond, interpreted in a stereotypically racialistic fashion.[7]

The residual power of the North/South dichotomy is now more than four centuries old. In studying this long and complex historical process some warning flags must be raised. Monocausality offers an alluring appeal, but it is only through multiple causes coming together that such enormous change can take hold so deeply and so enduringly. One must also be on guard against a belated historical perspective, one that views the processes of differentiation as being centred in the eighteenth century, where indeed an important flowering does seem to have occurred. But the genuine origin of this division reaches back discernibly into the sixteenth century where the combined[8] processes of decline and supersession had begun to take shape. This means that the North/South divide may be studied as a "sequence of linked ideas" and events, but it is also possible to go even further, and to examine it as a convergence of these groups of thoughts.[9] Processes that began in the sixteenth century – for instance, the expansiveness shown by Christian liberty – contained the seeds of what would inevitably be applied in a wider social and political context (e.g., civil liberties). The impetus and implications of their origins were evident, causing Erasmus to regret his prior participation in the establishment of Christian liberty, but which Coleridge celebrated when almost three centuries later he drew parallels between Luther and Rousseau (*Dualisms* 201–2). There are such interconnections to be observed.

This study of the Great Divide relies upon the convergence of three component parts. While not quite materialistic history, these three parts make it at least different from idealistic history. They are: first, the various staggering stories of decline, with causes so easy to enumerate, but in their profusion so hard to explain; second, the new issues introduced by the great phalanxes of Protestantism – the civil strife and the interminable divisions; and lastly, four telling concepts over which the rival parties quarrelled and warred, and which underwent their own crucial transformations, leading the way in that great transformation from the religious principles of the sixteenth century to the secular rights of the eighteenth. These three parts, while discussed separately, are not to be thought of as parcels of separate volumes; they are marked not by divergence but by convergence into a composite whole. By acting together as an ensemble they form the argument which sets forth the North/South divide.

(1) It is all too obvious that there could not be so potent and long-lasting a division without the transfer of empire (*translatio imperii*), the decline, for example, of Italy and Spain which in their losses came to epitomize the stagnant, unforthcoming nature of the South. It is startling to realize that their early historical impediments are still vestigially present to thwart their contemporary progress. Consequently, shortfalls in their responses to the crises of their times call for attention. The North/South divide would not have been what it was without the fall of these and other advancing empires in their turn. Decline seems to accompany any change in the organizations of nations. Once-powerful states become bases of repression and regression recognized as such even by themselves and well-placed visitors. Decline is shocking and on the mind. It does not pass unrecognized or unlamented. In most cases it is decisive and unrelieved. In the case of Italy, it endured long-lasting subjugation, and in Spain, there was periodic foreign control. But the demise of a state, unlike that of a human organism, is not tantamount to an absolute death. In our contemporary world, such powers, once toppled, even if they never totally recover, neither do they drop to the bottom; countries that had come to represent the South, while having relinquished their once primary stations, do not descend to the level of third world nations.[10]

Yet they have no chance of regaining their former status. To be sure, there are momentary signs of resurgence along the way, seeming to offer hope, but these flicker and dim once again as the downward spiral deepens. (China, while not a part of this study, seems to be an eminent exception.) However much the ruling bodies may contribute to their own demise, they have also been rudely pushed along their downward spiral. This is more like a playground slide, where eager nations jostle ahead to climb the rungs of power, where one or more resurgent powers – the northern provinces of the Netherlands, the United Kingdom, and France, and later other candidates – came to fulfil in unison and in competition the functions of a Northern ascendancy.

Later witnesses can with some authority and clarity identify the participants in this great European struggle. The roster of entries from the early modern period was clearly recognized by John Stuart Mill writing in *On Liberty* (1859).[11] For Mill the triumph of liberty – the nineteenth-century version of the recurrent hope of The End of History – is far from secure, and he lists the virtual elimination of dissident religious movements from the Vaudois (Waldensians) through the Lollards and the Hussites, before coming to the nation states that he lists together, as if forming a bloc, where liberty had been suppressed and persecution had become rampant: Italy, Spain, and despite locations not particularly southern, Flanders, and the Austrian-Hapsburg empire (97). Each in their different times and various ways could be considered bastions of the Southern mentality.

It was Voltaire who understood fully this great geographic divide, and who in one of his *contes philosophiques, La Princesse de Babylone*, explains what qualities are shared by the countries of the North.[12] Mistakenly alienated lovers in search of each other fly over the Northern tier of Europe, from the Russia of Catherine the Great (so-named despite an unfavourable European press that accused her not only of usurpation but also – falsely – of the death of her husband Peter III)[13] to the United Kingdom, and all the countries in between. Voltaire uses this device to explain the appeal of the Northern countries, and in so doing indicates his own social and political thought, its basis in moral philosophy and practical politics. The monarchs, generally enlightened and instructed in reason and philosophy, adhere to a *morale universelle*. They exhibit tolerance and provide havens for dissidents. Catherine, in extending her growing empire, offers freedom of religion to the southerners (*meridiens*, Islamists) who have been incorporated into the growing Empire (*Romans et contes* 384). The first law of the land is tolerance for all the religions. Prussia is included but its talented Emperor, Frederick II, is here eschewed, perhaps out of personal pique on Voltaire's part. The United Provinces are noted for liberty, equality, propriety, abundance, and tolerance. The countries that offer such collective freedoms seem to be thriving. In practical terms the United Kingdom survived the most terrible history of centuries of dynastic conflict, civil war, and Papal interference to emerge with (*"peut-être"*) the most perfect government on earth. It establishes the model shared by the other countries of a division of power, and an abhorrence of absolutism. Nobles and bourgeois share power (this in 1763) with the monarch – Catherine argued cogently that they were "limited monarchies." The decline of metaphysical jargon has helped focus on clear thinking (Bacon and Locke intended as models of rational thought but not mentioned). This balance of powers and the multiplicity and variety of religious sects, oddly enough, contributed to the peace and welfare of the country (one power degenerates into tyranny; two into cut-throat internecine warfare). All of the groups combine their varieties of religious belief to produce industry, commerce, and opulence. From this survey of the north of Europe, Voltaire is able to present his understanding of why the North seems to be living in some measure of freedom and affluence, with the great tolerance for varieties of religious opinion allowing for commercial success.[14]

(2) The second area necessary to the creation and understanding of the Great Divide is the emergence of new arguments. Invariably these grew out of or acquired new potency as a result of the Protestant Reformation. It is once again all too obvious that one cannot think of a North/South divide without the spread of Protestantism. Mme de Staël combines the two effectively: "Enfin ce qui donne en général aux peuples modernes du nord un esprit plus philosophique qu'aux habitants du midi, c'est la religion protestante que ces peuples ont presque tous adoptée" (Generally, what gives the people of the North more of a philosophical spirit than those of the South is the protestant religion which the [Northerners] have almost all adopted; *De la littérature* 186).[15] Beginning with the sixteenth century, a new ferment stirred the European pot, that of religious controversy. This produced a witches' brew of increased intensity and added hatred and hostility. It was from the pressure of this new force that the division acquired its cogency - the North characterized as predominantly Protestant, and the South as Catholic, yielding a new axial polarity. No country of western Europe (although it certainly touched central and eastern Europe as well) was spared the bitter fruit of this new source of antagonism. Enmity brought years of conflict, with bloody warfare waged between countries as well as internally, as countries individually tried to resolve the problems presented by two states, or two irreconcilable, militant religions within one nation, with the additional complications of the commingling of Church and State. The origin of the North/South divide tracks with the emergence of the various wings of Protestantism. The establishment of the very same principles that were the occasion of such conflict offered at the same time creative possibilities for new social solutions. Indeed, the sixteenth century that saw such religious conflicts arise (certainly abetted if not controlled by the usual dynastic and territorial motives

for warfare) also witnessed the emergence of forces that eventually brought such conflicts to an end.

One can read the events of the time as effecting a fracture in European Christian unity, but the changes may also be seen as instances of regeneration. One could argue that the function of this still embryonic but developing enlightenment was to render irrelevant and obsolete the theological and confessional reasons for conflict and to effect a separation between Church and State. D'Alembert and Mme de Staël were quick to note this theological decompression. Mme de Staël cites the historical change: "Que nous font à présent les plaisanteries sur les juifs ou sur la religion catholique! Le temps en est passé" (273; What do these witticisms about Jews or Catholicism have to do with us now? Their time has long passed). But even when the virulence of religious opposition had abated somewhat, the imprint of earlier antagonisms remained strong and divisions only widened, taken over by other social forces and phobias. And here the point of the argument is revealed. This very persistence within changing circumstances, its very diffusion and growth in intensity, makes manifest the thesis that the division between North and South is the most enduring, extensive, and meaningful development for a major part of the modern world, and that the early ruling spirit of this changing world resided primarily in the nature of Protestantism and the transformations that it promoted from seeds to sprouts to diverse fruit. While there is an observable difference between the acorn and the oak, there is also an undeniable lineage.

As Garrett Mattingly so accurately wrote, the Second World War was a war of great systems of ideas in conflict, so the inexorable collision of Spain and England was one to be sure of remarkably contrasting personalities, but also one where challenging systems of ideas met in mortal combat (*The Armada* v). These conflicting ideas will provide the warp to the woof of the material changes in the status of nations. One purpose of this study is to follow the transformations and continuities that led from the Renaissance and Reformation to the Enlightenment and beyond, or put another way, to follow the various roles of religion in the formation of the modern world. This is the true purpose of Max Weber's contested *The Protestant Ethic and the Spirit of Capitalism*, but even staunch and justified defenders of his thesis writ large shy away from addressing his mechanism of change, Calvinist predestination.[16] Clearly in the alchemy of religious change this hypothesis has its merits: one needs to show signs of election. We might be quite ready to find attractive the fabulous notion that Benjamin Franklin was the spiritual descendant of Calvin (an even more triumphant candidate marking a greater step along the way might be John D. Rockefeller, Sr, who believed God had placed him on earth to make money and whose ledger was his Bible) or even to accept the generalized modern mantra that "greed [or some variant] is good," and that this era of great change witnessed the modern acceptance of acquisitiveness as a striking replacement for the disallowed *cupiditas* of the Middle Ages.

(3) We owe much closer attention, however, to the actual ideas or concepts over which the North and South met in combat. There are four such points of intellectual disagreement, warring ideas, or lead ideas that help define the emergence of the North and the subjugation of the South, each of them originating in or acquiring added intensity through the Protestant Reformation. They are, as indicated above in the Preface, *Christian liberty*, *scepticism* (Christian or secular*), tolerance*, and *time*. The two contextual frameworks indicated above – the decline of nations and the various wings of Protestantism – are valuable and valid means for understanding the deepening North/South divide, but the major focus of this study will be the exploration and expansion of the four lead ideas. They differ in the roles that they played and in substance from the more material arguments. It has been observed that once a pre-eminent nation suffers a decline it rarely re-emerges to regain its former position. Protestantism, to consider an example of a movement, also has its limitations, beset by the splintering effects that Erasmus was among the first to identify and decry. In the quest for ideological purity, sectarianism prevailed, as one group of religious believers would break off from former partners in belief. Thus, Congregationalists differed from Presbyterians. Nations enjoy limited periods of hegemony, never to be quite as powerful as they once were. Sects break up to form other sects, and are distinguished by their emphasis upon differences in position. While nations once paramount fell into decline, religious groups easily set off on their own, their overriding focus not being conjunction and commonality but rather the proliferating separatist politics of difference.

But the four lead ideas are not troubled by these deficiencies – they are transformative. The appreciation of their character and engagement will constitute the major contribution of this volume. These "lead ideas" are formative principles, conveyor ideas that lead the way into the future and go far in providing the philosophical underpinnings of the actions and issues of the day. They possess continuity. They both transform and are transformed. They determine directions of thought.

Their value will be demonstrated by several major thinkers whose contributions represent milestones along the road of their development. They also enter into alliances, some long-lasting, some short-lived. Thus, the discussion of Christian liberty, for example, will be linked with a chapter on time, with which it shares some interests. Evidence for some awareness of a North/South divide in the sixteenth century is provided by texts from Machiavelli and Erasmus; more widely sweeping accounts rooted in climatology come from Jean Bodin and Giovanni Botero – both dating to the latter half of the sixteenth century. Their arguments are included not because they are convincing but because of their certainty regarding differences between the North and the South. The discussion relating to climate is followed by a review of Hegel's masterful treatment of Luther and the Reformation, and the more advanced understanding of Christian liberty and of the independent nature of liberty itself which follow. The argument then steps back to explore a different philosophical tradition, that of Milton and John Locke, in order to show how the original Christian concept became the basis for any succeeding discussion of civil liberties. In Milton's lexicon, being English meant one had to be a reformist Protestant. This will be followed by brief explorations of the views of Voltaire and Rousseau, before coming to the work of John Stuart Mill where the transformations of the original conception become clearer and its ultimate purpose is revealed. This potential spread and development of civil liberty was always implicitly present in Christian liberty – but it is the missing link in Weber's thesis. It should be made clear that in order to treat these varied concepts fairly in their relative contexts this essay will be obliged to loop back on itself before bringing them all together into a coherent whole.

All four of the concepts blossomed under challenging conditions. They both stood for and manifested great capacities for change, they were harbingers of the future. Unlike the collapsed nations which could not see beyond their past glories, the four concepts did not define themselves by their beginnings or endure a stasis. Each one changed, but still within certain confines. They were all ambitious ideas and showed themselves able to come into play in new contexts. Christian liberty led the way towards religious liberty and civil liberty. Scepticism became a procedural option and even acquired a dramatic voice ("Since no man knows aught of what he leaves, what is't to leave betimes? Let be"; *Hamlet* 5.2.169–70). It participated fully in the appeal for tolerance, and tolerance itself found its purpose in protecting religious minorities and dissidents, and going well beyond in the twentieth century to secure rights for groups, peoples, and nations. The concept of time was rediscovered as a new argument for Renaissance activism and, together with its adoption by the Reformation, contributed to the essential dynamic of the Northern countries. In the twentieth century time's own nucleus was transformed and this new understanding of time became one of the *points de départ* for literary modernism.

These, then, are the three intersecting, and mutually interacting areas to be explored: the essential progress, expansion, and consolidation of a North/South division, involving the parallel and reciprocal rise and fall of nation states; the shifting confessional balance resulting in Protestants finding their havens in the North and Catholics holding to their centres in the South; and the four basic concepts over which and through which debate was engendered. There are, of course, other ways of understanding the profound changes taking place in the cultures of Europe and beyond: through Max Weber's emphasis on Calvinist predestination, or as a quarrel between Ancients and Moderns (a tired subject injected with new life in Maravall's exhaustive study),[17] but the melding of these three areas seems to locate the argument where it ought to be – in the large and the small, in the micro- and the macrocosm, in the broad, sweeping geographic relocations, in the rise and fall of empires, and in the concepts over which and through which they individually struggled. Such multilayered causes are to be expected where people, places, and issues converge.

Here again two figures occupy defining positions, rather like bookends, with Erasmus as the representative of intellectual life at the first tentative emergence of the North/South divide, and Voltaire the representative who observes the culmination of the division. *North/South*, with all of its various facets, will continue to feature powerful thinkers (in addition to those already mentioned) pathfinders, consolidators, or exponents who gave the fullest expression to a particular issue or point of view. Not all were intellectuals, or writers; there were also great statesmen: think of William I, the prince of Orange, Oliver Cromwell, Gustavus Adolphus, and William III, whose great tasks were to hold parties and nations together and to seek alliances that would protect their people. Even among nations, this was an age – the early modern – in which populations required and sought after justification for change, religious change, and political change. It was also an age in which powerful forces throughout society resisted all change, both intellectual and political. Each of the contending parties becomes part of a permanence within genuine historical alterations, a permanence in practice, a dominance that holds its place.

The first major indication of the coming geographic realignment is observable in its transferral beyond Europe almost *in toto* to the developing northern and southern hemispheres of the "new world." The northern hemisphere, adopting ideas from Locke, was guided by the great minds that wrote the US Declaration of Independence, the Constitution and its amendments, and the adaptations that the Virginia men (Jefferson, Madison, Mason, and others) brought to their own state's leadership in the complex arguments attending the separation of Church and State, civil liberties, religious freedom, and freedom of speech. The great North/South divide is promoted in particular through the amazing technological development of the northern countries, revealed in the ingenious mechanical inventions of the industrial revolution. Spain, however, notoriously had little interest in or capability for mechanical technology. Italy, while its fertility in science continued, had long before used up its capital resources in luxury expenditures. The birth of the American experiment occurred at a time of great technological innovations, thus wedding inseparably American democracy and technological progress – usually associated with Anglo-American-Dutch virtues (more economically referred to as Anglo-Saxon qualities). The material means for the continuing expansion of the North were thus provided. But so, too, were the intellectual means: philosophers such as Hegel offered profound psychological insights and laid out paths for future explorations; the work of Max Weber, like that of his compeer William James, stressed the historical continuity between the religious issues of an earlier age and the social and intellectual developments of the modern world. This is a study in *géographie symbolique*, the attributes that are attached to place, and the complex causes for them.

The twentieth century was to endure yet a second dynamic change, involving a partial redefinition of the nature of the great North/South divide. Just as it was during the initial emergence of the great divide, when the fortunes of the North and those of the South were not independent of one another, so it is in this somewhat more recent redefinition, the two realities – a declining North and a reviving South – are not unrelated. This is not a zero-sum game. The long-standing growth and sustainability of the Northern experience began to show some fragility. This occurred also in the minds of its most representative figures, members of the intellectual caste. This fragility was met and furthered by a new advancement of the South, a new *prise de conscience*. The South, long accustomed to being discounted, began to rouse itself, spread its wings, and defend its virtues. After centuries the voices of the South, emerging from silence or obsequiousness, from being merely *porte-paroles* for the reigning Northern interests, found themselves empowered to define their own roles and values. In many countries throughout the world, the playing field was being levelled; or, at the very least, gaps in income and power were showing more flexibility and were not so heavily exaggerated in favour of the ascendant power. This means that countries other than Italy and Spain could be used as examples, but for reasons of space, ease of reference, and because of access to their already well-documented histories of decline, the signs of resurgence can be more closely followed through the countries already present within the confines of this study. In chapter 10 the contributions of this newly emergent "movement" will be assessed.

With the exception of the considerations indicated above and the discussion of the conflict with the Huguenots in France, this volume focuses on the stories of conflict between nations. Its main concern (as indicated in the Preface, vii) will be the pre-industrialized world and the forces and issues that dominate in contests between nations. It pays but passing attention to great industrial developments, such as the conflict between manufacturers and labour unions. Briefly, at its close, this study will point out some instances of continuity between the two historical moments, citing examples from Elizabeth Gaskell's *North and South* (1855), a section of George Orwell's *The Road to Wigan Pier* (1937), and selected pages from Eric Hobsbawm's three volumes devoted to the "long" nineteenth century. These works allow a glimpse of life within the worlds of capitalism, factories, industry, and empire, the consummate world towards which the North was both promising and promoting the ways.

Chapter Two

Decline and Resistance

The defeat of Spain ... was part of the wider defeat of Southern Europe by the North.

J.H. Elliott

There is mind and there is matter. And intellectual evaluations, despite their import, cannot stand alone but necessarily involve material realities as well. Certainly one cause of the formation of the North/South divide must be found in the decline of nations, which were bound to be swept aside in the transfer of Empire. One could of course join in the fun and humorously survey *The Decline and Fall of Practically Everybody*, as did Will Cuppy in a work that was doubtless more humorous when it appeared (1950) than it is now. But true decline, examplary decline, requires a fall from pre-eminence. The way poets are drawn to mortality and mutability, so historians are moved to seek out the causes of decline. And like poets, we meet with things dying and things new born, with lines that are falling and lines that are rising. Just as in a graph, such lines transect and places are exchanged. The transfer of Empire is a staggering principle of change.

Italy and Spain are the two agonists caught in this process in the sixteenth century, the first suffering total collapse, and the second beginning its long spiral of descent. There are many observable indications of both Spain and Italy's loss of pre-eminence. Whether they are effects or causes does not matter, because death can be attributed just as easily to secondary effects (pneumonia); symptoms can swing the wrecking ball. Despite shared ambitions the conditions of Italy and Spain were quite different. Spain emerged as the most potent European power in the sixteenth century. Italy's leadership was both cultural and economic; while not territorial, its ascendancy was imperial enough that its fall registers heavily on any social Richter's scale.

There is some disagreement over the *reasons* for Italy's economic decline. Carlo Cipolla attributes the slippage to high value Italian fabrics being undersold by the less costly textiles of the North, those cheaper to produce.[1] To allow a quip from today's globalized market, "They wanted Giorgio Armani at Walmart prices." So tight was the guild structure that Italian industry refused to bend to the more "mass" produced objects of the North. Italian products were more artful, akin to *objets d'art*. Hobsbawm tentatively agreed with Cipolla but would have liked to have seen more evidence ("The Crisis of the Seventeenth Century," in Aston 20). Yet Cipolla does describe a pattern of Italian manufacturing technique that is observed in the production of other products as well. The Italian lead in horology yielded to the Northern watch makers, who built less artful but more saleable time pieces (Cipolla, *Clocks and Culture* 53–4).[2] David Landes in his *Revolution in Time* places this development in a North/South confessional context. Despite the temporal concerns of intellectuals like Dante, Petrarch, and Alberti, "by the late sixteenth century, the typical watch wearer was North European and Protestant" (92). With respect to ordnance, the story is a mixed one, but on the whole the lead in the manufacture of cannon shifted to the larger nations. They commanded more troops in the field who could more handily manoeuvre larger weapons, and they produced weaponry that was more mobile and easier to reload. One of the major obstacles to any effective Italian response to its competition may have been its regulatory system of guilds. According to Hobsbawm, however, who allies himself with a Marxist position, Italy was not prepared for the expenditure of capital required to meet the needs of industrialization; instead it allotted its capital to buildings and luxury items. Italy was de-industrialized before it could even be industrialized. While Hobsbawm argues that the problem was generalized, provoking the "crisis" of the seventeenth century in Europe, when countries were not strong enough to break free of their social framework (28), the question remains why some of the countries – the northern Protestant ones – were eventually able to overcome what he calls the "social framework."

There are major material causes for the decline of Italian humanism, for its fall from its position at the centre of culture. These material causes have mainly to do with geography, politics, and the presence of the Papacy as a deciding power in Italy. Italy was a decentralized, fragmented assortment of city-states, republics, and principalities. Writers from Dante to Machiavelli complained constantly regarding the Papacy's intrusion into Italian politics. The Papacy was not strong enough to unify Italy but it was strong enough and clever enough to prevent any one Italian state from unifying the various regions. For Machiavelli, whose reasoning I have been paraphrasing, the Papacy was the dog in the manger. Its self-defensive policies that blocked unification left the door open for foreign invasions. He even postulates that if you could take a cleanly and efficiently run state like Switzerland and introduce the papal court – the Curia then as now taking its blows – in no time at all, you would have all kinds of disorder and poor practice take root that could not have arisen by any other means (*Discourses* I.xii, 55–6).

Despite Machiavelli's humorous slur and analysis, Rome had come to be regarded as *la capitale moderne de la république des lettres*.[3] When it was sacked in 1527 by the German and Spanish mercenaries, convulsive shock waves were felt throughout Europe. The height of its cultural ascendancy may be calibrated by the degree of dismay at its fall. The wasting of Florence followed in 1530. Such foreign domination, lasting until the Risorgimento of the nineteenth century, would obviously do much to dampen Italian spirits, and in particular would deprive Italian humanism of any energetic commitment of its learning to political, civic, and communal causes. Hence the findings of Milton and Voltaire in their descriptions of the dispirited Italians (see p. 26 below), and Voltaire's portrait of the languid Pococurante in *Candide*. The character of this man "who cares for little" has not been sufficiently addressed. Lacking a sense of liberty or even commitment, he has read all there is to read and his spirit is weak. Although Voltaire does not refer to liberty in his portraiture of this man, its absence is still felt.

Rome was called the eternal city not because it went undefeated or never was plundered but because after every vicissitude it managed to revive itself, and because on every era it managed to leave its mark – the city of seven hills was one of seven cultures. Like Rome itself the Papacy revealed the strengths and staying power of a powerful institution. Through the centuries from Boniface VIII, to Julius II, to Sixtus V, it showed an amazing capacity to revive after disaster. After the fiasco of the fourteenth and fifteenth centuries, and after the sack of Rome in 1527, it managed to produce powerful popes, spirited men rather than spiritual. Such was Sixtus, who was "formidable," "iron-willed," and who devoted his energies to rebuilding Rome, to making it into a modern city (Hughes 243). What Baron Haussmann was to Paris in the nineteenth century, Robert Moses to New York City in the twentieth, and later Mayor Daley to Chicago, Sixtus was to Rome. They all possessed the powers of mind and will to refashion their great city's environment according to the needs and values of their generation. Sixtus represented a modern muscular Christianity, and had no intentions of having his plans stopped out of reverence for pagan antiquity. He came to bring not peace but the sword, and with that sword he cut swaths though the ancient city (244). His was the proud and confident vigour that prompted churchmen of the early sixteenth century to refer to Luther and Erasmus (mistakenly) as antiquarian. As regards the antiquities of Rome, "he did not see why the remains of a defeated paganism should be allowed to impede the progress of a triumphant faith" (247). This rebuilding of Rome at the end of the sixteenth century was part of a larger Catholic counter-Reformation in the arts that we preferably term Baroque (which found its *chefs-d'oeuvre* by Caravaggio, Bernini, and Rubens in Rome and its political resurgence led by the Jesuits throughout Europe and the New World). The Church became a vast commercial enterprise, called by Milton "not a religion, but a Roman principalitie" (*A Treatise of Civil Power* 458).

When Dostoevsky printed his Grand Inquisitor prose-poem by Ivan in serial form, friends complained that the "attack" against religion was confusing because it seemed to give too many weapons having contemporary resonance to the enemies of religion. Dostoevsky advised them to hold their judgment until the full text was published (for a somewhat different take, see *Dualisms* 286–91). But there remained an elusive truth in this daring composition, and that was the recognition that the emergent earthly power of the Church, here represented by the Inquisition, had adjusted to the realities of the modern world and thus had no apparent need for the spirituality of Jesus. Like Milton in his depiction of Satan, Dostoevsky in the Grand Inquisitor may be perceived to be of the opposite party without knowing it. But this does not hold. Both Milton and Dostoevsky knew full well that they were describing a new, revolutionary assertion of pride and power, a formidable presence that can only be curtailed by a superior power; this power is present in their great works, but is made manifest primarily through acts of faith and brotherly love.

Christian liberty is a fearful calling – it can lead ultimately to "free thought and science." The return of Jesus with his doctrine of spiritual freedom is more than an embarrassment, it is an impediment to the more up-to-date and modern functioning of the Church. Dostoevsky is not inventing a fable he is rather recording compelling historical fact. These bold and brazen men saw in the Church a new and necessary order for society. Man was made for the sabbath and for mystery, miracle, and authority as well. These were their overwhelming convictions, and their responses to the challenges of Christian liberty and French socialism. They anticipated that the particular devastation of the latter would send people scurrying back to the comforting warmth and security of the Church. Dostoevsky writes in direct contradiction of those who claim that Christian liberty has no legacy, and condemns those who might have feared its introduction in the early years of the Reformation, and who would have suppressed it in the name of an autocratic theocracy.

The world, according to the beliefs of the Grand Inquisitor, has been divided into the ten per cent who govern and assume the burdensome façade of religious faith and the slavish remainder who follow. These pseudo-leaders have weathered all the storms, and will continue to do so, because they know human nature. They know the sixteenth century's reformed versions of freedom, what it means to be in the hands of the living god, and the nineteenth century's revolutionary fervor. While not possessing the energy of Sixtus they still affirm his vision and know that they will survive, adopting a Christianity of political and social controls that was a Christianity without Christ. The genius of this powerful selection from *The Brothers Karamazov* derives from Dostoevsky's argument with the nineteenth century as being a perverse detachment from the advent of Christian liberty as brought about in the sixteenth. The Church was a secular institution (or industry) that offered people the security they needed rather than the spiritual freedom they thought they wanted. The spokesman is the disappointed idealist, Ivan, but the creative genius is that of Dostoevsky who saw so deeply into the historical and emotional natures of humankind.[4]

Unlike Italy, Spain was an imperial power, the most formidable land power of Europe. By 1580 it had added Portugal and its holdings to its control; it held Sicily as well as Naples and Milan on the Italian peninsula; and from the Hapsburg succession of Charles V acquired the Netherlands – a fateful and costly bequest. The home of intrepid voyagers and adventurers it also had its extremely productive overseas colonies. The march of its *tercios* made cities tremble and in the southern Netherlands the rampage of the *furia espagnole*, slaughtering entire populations, gave rise to the deserved *leyenda negra*. But already in the sixteenth century, contemporary analysts begin to detect chinks in its armor, discernible even in the rigidly stiff designs it produced, so different from the French neo-classical productions that Georges Jacob designed for the court of Louis XV1 at Versailles: the one seemingly committed to militancy and the other contoured for physical comfort; or consider the contrast of El Escorial with Versailles, the former influenced by the ascetic temperament of Philip II, committed to a monastic-like militancy, while the latter still recalls Rabelais's Abbaye de Thélème (founded on principles of *libre volonté, Gargantua* LII).

Spain suffered from the classic symptoms of a nation in decline: a bloated bureaucracy, over-extended military commitments, and the necessary recourse to burdensome taxation on a shrinking population. To these symptoms, Spain contributed its own particulars: a *hidalguia* that blanches at the prospect of productive labour, depopulation caused by famine and plague, the infamous expulsions of useful craftsmen, of middle-men (the *conversos* in 1492 and the *moriscos* in 1609), and the evident neglect of those who cannot claim *limpieza de sangre*, leading to the promotion of those who could still lay claim to purity of bloodline, however meager their abilities. The bullion from Mexico and Potosi certainly helped the regime's coffers but this income was not put to productive use, and its transfer to Spain constantly ran the risk of interception by privateers. With its lack of productivity – Spanish character was never greatly interested in industry or technology (the Venetian ambassador to Spain reported, "I do not believe there is another country less provided with skilled workers than Spain" – quoted in Cipolla, *Guns, Sails and Empires* 33), its treasure from abroad easily passed into the hands of the German and Genoese bankers, the Fuggers and Dorias, and other more industrious profiteers. Spain was "poor in its riches." "Easy money is bad for you" (Landes, *The Wealth and Poverty of Nations* 173). Baron de Montesquieu explains in a brief section of *De l'Esprit des Lois* why it was not easy money but rather a hard monetary system that led to the "misery" of Spain. What European observers could not suspect was that the gold and silver brought back from the Americas constantly lost a portion of its value, while the goods that the Spaniards sought to purchase were on a rising curve of value. This financial trap led to the first bankruptcy of Phillip II, and Montesquieu's stern judgment, "Depuis ce temps, la monarchie d'Espagne declina sans cesse"

(Bk. 21, ch. 22; From this time forward the Spanish monarchy began its endless decline). So extensive are the lists of Spain's weaknesses that one can begin to wonder how it came about that Spain was the most feared European power for a hundred years. One hundred years in the making, it took more than a hundred years to reach its decline and fall (Hamilton).[5] With all these accumulating defects the real question should be, how it endured at all and for so long. In a brilliant essay, so thorough in uncovering hidden corners of Spanish life, Felipe Fernández-Armesto, after winnowing out all the *pro* and the *con* reasoning behind Spain's rise and fall, summarizes the paradox perfectly: "The fragility of the subject is always apparent, its durability always impressive" ("The Improbable Empire" in Carr 117).

The history we are following is one of decline and fall but also one of emergence. In the grand scheme of world politics, where one nation falls, others arise. Just as a nation does not gain ascendancy by default, so in its fall it is acted upon by powerful forces of supersession. The fundamental principle remains the facts of historical change, facts that call for new and different responses. Other countries, those coming to the fore, may be seen in contrast as responding to a changing world, or perhaps more accurately were themselves the agents of change. It is an all-too-obvious but still astonishing fact that as the fates of Italy and Spain were being sealed the settlements in North America were just commencing. The writing was on the wall, but it took several hands to fully convey the message.

In the concluding pages of *Europe Divided 1559–1598*, John H. Elliott describes some of the critical differences that exacerbated the widening gap between the Catholic South and the Protestant North. In his analysis, it was Protestantism that by the end of the sixteenth century produced "a new and recognizable breed of leaders of society." Protestant church life itself encouraged "individual participation" and collective decision-making through discussion (267) – as well as, importantly, respect for individual conscience. Constitutionalism, "a contractual relationship between the ruler and the ruled ... [i.e.,] political liberty ... became a necessary precondition for liberty of mind" (268). Similarly, liberty of cult became a precondition for liberty of conscience. These realizations, birthed in the midst of conflict, were matters of fact before they became articles of faith or subjects of treatises (267).

Indications of more extensive change became apparent, beyond that which transformed the lives of individuals. Early signs were provided by the "shift in emphasis" from the Mediterranean, the "great middle sea," so rich in its multitudes of city-ports, to the Atlantic North. There were also signs of a more productive energy. "In these Northern societies, a new dynamism was detected, as they began to acquire certain recognizable characteristics of their own." Elliott lists these qualities: "a degree of political representation and political liberty, an insistence on the high priority to be given to commercial activity and business enterprise, a concern for precision and exact observation, and a modified acceptance of intellectual and religious dissent," evidence pointing to the conclusion that "already by 1600 there were hints of a growing divergence of character between those societies and those of southern Europe" (268).

David Landes, in *The Wealth and Poverty of Nations* (1998), where he strongly defends the classic thesis of Max Weber, reaches similar conclusions: the advances made by the North over the South "attracted notice." This was "already" the case in the eighteenth century, he remarks somewhat tardily; he does not name the commentators who were drawn to this division, but his contentions are sound. On the "empirical level" he notes that Protestants played a "leading role in trade, banking and industry." Max Weber remarks quite early on "the smaller participation of Catholics in the modern business life of Germany ..."; he also refers to a similar disproportion among those attending institutions of higher learning and, at the other extreme, "among the skilled laborers of modern industry." On the theoretical level, Landes points to the formation of a "new kind of man – rational, ordered, diligent, productive" (177).

There were contemporary theories for the superiority of the North over the South. Among the most prevalent (but entirely inadequate) were theories of the effects of climate on personality. From Jean Bodin and Giovanni Botero in the sixteenth century, down to Baron de Montesquieu in the eighteenth century, observers saw in climate one of the causes behind the separation of North and South. Climatologists like Bodin and Botero were in need of the corrective of Milton's much later observation in *Paradise Lost* that all the previous great epics were composed in warmer climes and to take note of his fears about not being able to complete his great epic in a "cold/Climate" (*Paradise Lost* ix. 43–6). More detailed discussion in chapter 6 will show how it was Bodin and Botero themselves who inadvertently revealed the various fallacies of climatology. It would take Voltaire to state explicitly that the real objects of study and the true subjects of change are nations and persons and issues or religion and principles of government. What the geography of the North offered was hospitality not causality – a hospitable political environment for the free development of thought, of conscience, and of *cult* (all in somewhat limited doses). Mme de Staël does credit climate as *one* of the "*raisons principales*" for differences between the North from the South (179), but the subtitle of her study of literature is "in relation to (its) social institutions." Climate is thus considered alongside race, religion, and government (or types of regulating agencies). Cultural geography means that geography is only symbolic, a necessary place, possibly correlative and if causative, only partially so.

One other characteristic from Elliott's tablet of differences is "dynamism," borrowed via Cassirer. It is a difficult term to define, but not to illustrate. It indicates a capacity to foster change as well as a willingness to encounter new ideas. It bespeaks a fundamental faith that is willing to accommodate newness and even deviations. The Northern countries seemed to exhibit and move forward with such dynamism, while the Southern countries seemed to stagnate, to fall victim to desiccation. Fernández-Armesto notes a demoralization, rather than an influx of dynamism, overtaking Spanish society from the 1590s (Carr 145).

Dynamism is a state of mind; where it is present, fatalism, intellectual narrowness, fear, and oppression are deplored. Dynamism has no need of Seville's Inquisition or Rome's Index. It strikes a winning attitude, a searching confidence, and independence. Unconscious of its own resources, it is more like an instinct, an animal energy, and faith; its coming and goings are unaccountable, except that its absence leads invariably to stagnation. More than a half-century later Milton presents a discouraging picture of the Italian humanists who are without civic or cultural freedom and commitments. They themselves bemoan the servile condition to which they have been brought by the Council of Trent, and Milton regrets that the "glory of Italian wits" was so dampened that they could produce nothing but "flattery and fustian" (*Areopagitica* 306). Likewise, Voltaire writes with some bewilderment to his trusted Italian colleague, Francesco Algarotti, wondering that there be such men who would seek to prevent other men from reading. He predicts that in the future people will find it hard to believe that such a restriction could have prevailed. Italy, "the most ingenious nation on the earth, is like an eagle having its wings clipped by screech owls" (*Correspondence* 53, 85).

Despite the opposition of formidable enemies, many of the wounds that Italy and Spain received were self-inflicted. There are those for whom time is a heavy burden, and others for whom its newness represents an acceptable challenge. The former chose the way of the Index following the Council of Trent, which determined the path of the counter-Reformation, while Spain became notorious for the Inquisition, which was anathematized (only with some exaggeration) by the majority of the thinkers (William, Prince of Orange, among the earliest, Milton, Locke, Voltaire, and Rousseau, see below). For his conciliatory efforts Erasmus earned the honour of having all of his programmatic works placed at the head of the list of prohibited books. Milton's *Paradise Lost* made the list in 1700. What this means is that Italy and Spain had choices to make, and for whatever reasons – and they were many – they chose the path of fidelity to the Catholic church and to what they construed to be their ways of life. They had an historical burden to assume, while the North had their ancient liberties and present existence. It is not as if the Spaniards were unaware of their problems. Vives addresses the economic dimension: "Awareness of economic crisis, which spread through Spain at the moment of its greatest political splendor, was general around 1600 ("The Decline of Spain in the Seventeenth Century," see Cipolla 32). Somewhere between apprehension of a crisis and the action needed to address the problem a crippling paralysis of the will is encountered. This is an emotional weight that is hard to dispel, and involves the deepest aspects of the human personality. Out of some emotional neediness, an unwillingness, an incapacity to change when change was required (perhaps amounting to a choice without a choice) brought down the advanced learning of Italy and the military might of Spain. Given the choice between reason and honour, they chose a debilitating faith and loyalty, and this quite consciously, opening a downward spiral to degeneration and decay. In Spain, as many including Vives have argued, the competent and commendable *arbitristas* quite accurately diagnosed their country's economic and political problems and advocated plausible solutions, but they were not heeded. In addition, Trent (the counter-Reformation) and Seville (the Inquisition), in order to contend with the rising tide of Protestantism, steadfastly built walls designed to protect their subjects from the intrusion of alien ideas, that is, truly insulated themselves against foreign contamination. They shut themselves off from the most liberalizing ideas of their time (an action that both Erasmus and Thomas More rejected). They nailed shut their doors to the future, and suffered from the consequent loss of rational energy, the capacity to move forward with some confidence. It should be recalled, however, in the midst of doom and gloom that the coming seventeenth century saw the great achievements of the Spanish Golden Age, represented by such figures as Lope de Vega, Cervantes, and Velasquez.

The Inquisition may have suffered from exaggerations of *la leyenda negra* that began quite early, and it can be shown that the actual number of executions and incidents of bodily torture were comparable with those in other countries, but as Camus has taught us, fear is a technique,[6] thriving in an atmosphere of collective timidity that succeeds in inhibiting any manifestation of bold action or independent thought. (One sparkling counterexample is the forthrightness of William, Prince of Orange in his *Apologia*, see below.) Fernández-Armesto, again correcting "vulgar" suppositions concerning the Inquisition, can nevertheless conclude that "in practice" its effect was "divisive and depressant," "spreading insecurity with its secretive procedures and vast web of informers, setting neighbors at loggerheads and inducing an atmosphere of fear" (in Carr 133).

Like the gulags in Stalinist Russia, which were not identical with the regime but were certainly expressive of its interests and programs, the Inquisition was expressive of a culture devoted to homogeneity, to a form of purification that quite easily came to symbolize the regime itself. Whether we are discussing a cause or a manifestation does not make much difference. The Inquisition's contributions to *la leyenda negra*, were substantial, though the discourse required no such assistance, given the activities of the Duke of Alba in the Netherlands. To be sure, *la leyenda* was a tool of Protestant propaganda, to which it lent itself so readily. But the klaxons of opprobrium were sincere and accurate as well. As with the gulags, the consequences of the Inquisition were irremediable. It is difficult to pinpoint the number of deaths, but when the numbers range between the high and low thousands, they are equally horrific. Yet what was clearly evident was its stifling effect on the culture of Spain, which once had been the most energetic and diverse in Europe. The scar on the body politic remains in the collective memory, the methods of death, the torture, and the burnings at the stake, all within public view and, we gather, with some approval. Where the Inquisition prevailed the four substantive concepts were quashed. At first designed to keep alien ideas out, and to prevent such contaminations from breaching the walls of the city, it soon became a wall designed to keep its people in, a form of mental imprisonment, where, under the programs of censorship and a cadre of informers and thought police, the wall worked to prevent people who were within from moving without, a kind of quarantine lasting longer than the prescribed time. Spain became a city besieged by itself.

All of these unhappy responses only served, as Elliott concludes, to separate Hapsburg Spain from the mainstream of European intellectual development. "Early sixteenth century Spain was Erasmian Spain ... From the 1550s there was a chilling change in the cultural climate" (Cipolla 188). The decline of Spain has attracted so much attention because, as Elliott has so astutely observed, "The defeat of Spain ... was part of the wider defeat of Southern Europe by the North."

Identifying the trigger for Spain's decline, particularly as it began so swiftly after reaching the pinnacle of its power and prestige in 1580, is no easy task. After airing all the causes of decline, and their well-known toxic effects, it is still unclear why Spain did little to address these problems. This might be because the making and the unmaking of Spanish hegemony were nearly simultaneous and are in fact bound together. The very means of Spain's success was to become the cause of its demise. To understand this, one must look to other psychic habits, the mental matrix out of which response is formed. Here it seems to speak of paralysis of action, a stymied will. Clearly character is key, but character in relation to circumstance. And in Spain's case one can see that the circumstances that Spain confronted called on aspects of its personality that were ill-equipped to deal with such problems. The Spanish – in their stiff-backed chairs – could not bend to the retrenchment required.

The various arguments used to explain the decline have one serious shortcoming. They assume that corrective actions can be taken that will substantially alter the long-term outcome. Searches for the causes of decline are ubiquitous. If all paradises are lost paradises, so all empires decline and finally fall. Both Dante and Shakespeare, whose understanding of change was not only wide in scope but intense in focus, provide the kind of philosophical understanding that would be useful here. (See *Purgatorio* X1 115–17, but I quote from Shakespeare.) The bowed and bloody Henry IV, despondent over the years of civil strife that his unseating of Richard II has been unable to quell, reflects upon the role of change in Nature and in human activities:

> O God, that one might read the book of fate,
> And see the revolution of the times
> Make mountains level, and the continent,
> Weary of solid firmness, melt itself

Into the sea …
… How chances mock
And changes fill the cup of alteration
With divers liquors.   (III.i.45–53)

Shakespeare's king, a sacred executioner, that is, one who must enter into ambiguous actions that nevertheless make way for peaceful resolutions, seems despondent (he is actually quite ill). But when advised that these changes affecting his regime are clear and explicable through an understanding of the issues involved, he gathers his forces and commits himself to meeting the demands with the energies required (for a contrast of the character of Henry IV with that of the Spanish monarchs, see Appendix).

This is of course one response, and perhaps even typical of the Elizabethans and their monarch. But languishing is another older response, one exposed by Augustine whose view, surveying the fates of earthly cities, is far more pessimistic. The earthly city may very well be the best thing going, but survival is not a given. If its victories provoke arrogance, then they are "life-destroying and short-lived." But even if its victories are marked by *pietas* (a concern for the "common casualties of our mortal nature") they are still only short-lived for the city "cannot abidingly rule over those whom it has victoriously subjugated" (*The City of God* XV.iv).[7] Augustine thus predicts hardship, toil, and eventual defeat even for those cities waging war in order to bring peace. This stems from what lies at the origins of the two cultures to which Augustine was heir (Roman and Hebrew): the controlling myths of each earthly city, the original stain of fratricide, from which it struggles to be cleansed.

When viewed against the enormity present in Dante's awareness of the disappearance of entire cities, and Shakespeare's consciousness of the destruction of the globe itself, any solutions proposed amount only to small steps of remediation, solutions to problems one can truly grapple with. But what if the problems are endemic, so profound and all-consuming that their historical fate must work its own way out, that there is not much to be done? The fall of an empire is so overwhelming, the manifestation of symptoms so pervasive, and so inextricably bound up with its virtues and successes, that in fact there is no remedy for decline, but the empire is condemned instead to a slow succumbing to inevitable displacement. One is better off searching for the reasons for its rise to pre-eminence, its accomplishments, and the brightness of the light it does shed on its contemporaries.

Religion and the Paths to Resistance

Just as the theme of decline runs through the arguments of this study, so do the various roles of religion. The wars of this time have been called "wars of religion" and in part they deserve that designation: religion both provoked battle and blocked the ways to peace.[8] But the total picture is more complex than that. For instance, the term "religion" involves a multitude of different denominational attitudes. There are obvious conflicts among Anabaptists, Zwingliites, Lutherans, and Calvinists over such matters as the Lord's Supper and the role of violent resistance itself. Moreover, religion was not the sole motivating factor in taking up arms. Obviously, the normal human motives – greed, ambition, self-interest, as well as dynastic and territorial disputes – issued their own calls to war. Alliances between super-powers and lesser forces had internal trip-wires; such alliances were condemned by Erasmus, Luther, and many others. It was just such a system of alliances among various powers that set off the last "unnecessary" war, the First World War.

Rulers and their councils brought into their alliances high-level geopolitical considerations in which religion was not a major concern. Philip II was warned about tying his fortunes too closely to those of the Papacy, while the Vatican chafed at its subordination to the powers of Spain. The interests of France brooked no hesitation in attacking the Holy See whether in 1494 or 1527. While publicly the Papacy deplored any victory of "Protestant" France, in private it could take some satisfaction in that prospect. At the end of the sixteenth century, France (where the Catholics outnumbered the Protestant Huguenots more than ten to one) joined with England and the United Provinces (each decidedly Protestant) in a northern alliance against Spain. The agile cardinal-minister Richelieu sided with the great "savior" of Protestantism in the North, Gustavus Adolphus. Richelieu's successor, Mazarin, had a distant working relationship with Oliver Cromwell, but an understanding aimed at protecting Catholics in the United Kingdom. These are only a few of the many examples showing the widespread cross-alliances that should temper any hasty condemnation of the so-called wars of religion. They may be assailed but not solely because of their religious content.

It is perhaps time to utter some unholy truths. There were some hidden benefits in these brutal conflicts. The first is that war breeds its own causes for termination. When war-weariness (*tedium belli*) sets in, when expenses grow too burdensome for the people, the fight is no longer worth the candle, and attacks on the civilian population become too horrific, other more creative alternatives are sought, such as reconciliation, unification, concessionary tolerance, even monetary pay-offs. War was instrumental in pushing Europe towards the culture and expectations of the Enlightenment. Hegel maintained that "In England war was indispensable to the establishment of the Protestant church" (*The Philosophy of History* 434). Odd as it might seem, those countries) that did not experience contention within of two nations, or two religions (such as Spain – see Fernández-Armesto in Carr 143), were the countries that could not open out onto the fields of regenerative thought and found themselves closeted socially, intellectually, and politically. It is a sad fact that bloodshed should be the salutary prescription that permits such transformation to take place.

These combats had far-reaching effects not only historically but also in the way they shaped the future relation of Europe to its most recent antagonist, Islam. Undoubtedly the aroused energies of the leading partisans (Lutheran, Calvinist, and Catholic) provided the moment and the situation that separated the West from Islam. This was the crucial period in which great differences asserted themselves. As Bernard Lewis has written, when Muslims survey the world they "tend to see not a nation subdivided into religious groups but a religion subdivided into nations" (*The Crisis of Islam* xx). The world that the West left behind was the one in which Islam remained. In entering this crucible of change the European West (at least the Northern tiers) separated itself from its medieval heritage as well. It was Christianity, as characterized by the four ideas indicated above (and discussed more fully below) that contained the seeds of this tremendous transformation.

Despite major differences regarding the use of political insurgency, the major Protestant sects traversed the same roads, had similar obstacles to overcome, and arrived at similar ends, passing the baton, so to speak – from Lutherans after the failure of the Diet of Augsburg, to the Huguenots after the massacre of St Bartholomew's day in 1572, to the resistance of the Calvinists in the Netherlands after the betrayal of Philip II in 1580. Quentin Skinner, in *The Age of Reformation*, follows in great detail these transformations; his stated goal is to survey the "foundations of modern revolutionary ideology." At first, the North was lacking the dedication to *libertà* so typical of the early Italian city-states and even principalities. The northern countries needed to evolve a theory of freedom, one that incorporated justification of action. This was rendered difficult by one overarching principle in their thinking: while they might argue for a separation between the things that belong to God and those that pertain to the earthly city, religious principle had a commanding hold of their entire existence. Consequently, their political bent was, on the whole, one of "quietism." They believed that their rulers – the king and magistrate – were ordained by God and thus not subject to human tampering or change. If the ruler was malevolent and vicious he or she would have to answer to God for their evil. A bad ruler can be regarded as punishment for the sins of the community. In another more modern translation, you get the kind of government you deserve.

I am merely devising here a general blueprint, in which the building details will differ according to the religious confessions. Through a series of steps – pushed along unawares but compelled by an inherent logic – their hesitancy to engage in revolution was gradually surmounted. Through the bitter cauldron of challenge, threats, and warfare itself, they were obliged to take up arms to remediate their conditions and thus had to overcome their religious scruples. Ideas grow out of conflict, where one is obliged to accept positions one had not at first anticipated. Thus Luther was brought to acknowledge that "we were all Hussites without knowing it" (*Dualisms* 63).

There were two major changes brought about by the very heated debates. First was the change in the object of ordination. Upon closer scrutiny it was decided that what God had anointed was not the individual holder of the office, but the office itself. Not to accept this distinction would be to impute human sin to the Godhead. Accordingly, the lower magistrate is practically and morally justified in defying and deposing the wicked monarch. Another even more powerful argument may be produced when the king or magistrate behaves so badly that he betrays and annuls the very office that he tends. He violates the very premises upon which his tenure depends, thus opening the way to his own removal.

So stated, the arguments seem theoretical, devoid of passion, and apparently unaware of the difficulties involved. Yet, it was a tremendous responsibility to resist or rebel against the deputy anointed by the Lord. One hindrance to rebellion that carried great weight was the notion of suffering persecution for righteousness sake. A radical change of heart was required before even the firm conviction that one was in the right could lead to insurrection. Skinner, tracing the arguments of resistance, uncovers the "modern and strictly political concept of a moral right to revolution" (II. 240). With some justification Skinner attributes primacy of influence to the Huguenot thinkers. "The result [of the abandonment of traditional arguments] is a fully *political* theory of revolution founded on a recognizably modern, secularized thesis about the natural rights and original sovereignty of the people" (II. 338). This theory was "taken over" by the Calvinists in the Northern provinces of the Netherlands, after which it entered into England and "came to form an important part of the intellectual background of the revolution of 1640" (II. 240). Thus, despite differences with Max Weber, Skinner follows the same path of emphasizing the essential contributions of religious justification and ideology to modern thought. Their intention is to highlight the great purpose uniting many of the writers of these chapters: it was out of the growth of their religious thought and development that the Protestant North led the way to secular freedom, to those liberties, civil and religious, that typified the Enlightenment.

But when one states this argument emphasizing only one side, immediately the question of the relevance of secular thought arises and there is some surprise that it should be an absent partner in revolutionary change. There are several reasons for this. First is the change in Italian thought itself. Once the beacon of *libertà*, the Italian city states, particularly Rome and Florence, underwent their own subjection to despotic rule. The great Francesco Guicciardini's thought veered towards the tragic, and to Hamlet's question "whether love lead fortune, or fortune love," from the play whose theme is the "overthrow" of all the "devices," the answer coming from the voices that once proclaimed the virtues of liberty now laments the rule of fortune and fate. That proud line of Florentine thought that led from Leonardo Bruni and his cohorts to Machiavelli and Guicciardini is faced with catastrophe and is of hardly any use to the Huguenots in France or to the rebellious forces in the Netherlands. Moreover, even when doctrines of republican liberty flowed freely, the forces that might have heeded them were committed to an enlightened monarchy.

When addressing aspects of German thought this dilemma is most apparent, involving as it does the Weberian thesis that elides and either eliminates or makes a caricature of Luther. Skinner's tendencies in the same direction do not give full credit to the efforts of the Lutherans. The evolution of a German theory of resistance is traced by Heinrich

Bornkamm, writing "that the problem of resistance against the Emperor had been under discussion for years" and "for the evangelicals the right to resist the Emperor became the major political theme during 1529" (*Luther in Mid-Career* 655). Martin Brecht, author of a three-volume biography of Luther, goes into minute detail covering the period 1531–2, (*Martin Luther* vol. 2: *Shaping and Defining the Reformation*), when Luther had at first defended the impermissibility of armed resistance to the Emperor. Such resistance would amount to placing "personal security" above a trust in God. This trust leads to a quietism, which is at the heart of the evangelicals' reluctance to take effective steps to ameliorate their conditions (Bornkamm 654–6). Political discussions of rebellion could not be separated from theological questions of faith and the nature of the Eucharist. The real danger came not from the Emperor or his magistrates but rather from Satan, the ruler of the world.

Methods of response were twofold: chastisement of sin or various degrees of resistance to oppressive overlords. Sin should be left in the hands of God, while malfeasance should be left to the arms of the Electors (whose very numbers, however, rendered actions difficult and complex). Charles V aggravated his own position and gave impetus to rebellion when he imprisoned the two emissaries who brought a petition from local authorities. According to "secular law," one may form defenses against an emperor who has broken his oath to attack no one nor to infringe on local freedoms. But for the Christian there is, according to a strict reading of Scripture, no such right to resistance (664–5). The distinction lies between sin and an act that is criminal or an abridgment of freedoms: the first one can denounce, but the second calls for some resignation. But this division in responses did not prevent Luther's dramatic actions from resonating down the halls of history, nor his more religious pronouncements from providing encouragement for secular actions.

These two arguments – action versus quietism and the different responses called for by sin and public action – become major themes in two of Shakespeare's greatest dramas: *Richard II*, introducing the issues that require the subsequent tetralogy to work themselves out, and *Hamlet*. It should not be surprising that contemporary theological and political issues are reflected in Shakespeare's dramas. They are keenly dramatic and on people's minds. In Shakespeare's second tetralogy (*Richard II*, *1 and 2 Henry IV*, and *Henry V)* the debates and actions between characters are motivated by these opposing ideas. The major one, introduced to the modern world by Machiavelli, advances the necessity and legitimation of rebellion. These new radical responses were shared by the beleaguered Protestant sects in Germany (around 1530) and later by religious groups in France and the Netherlands. While their premises, preoccupations, and debates are different, their end result is similar (one of the contemporaneous fruits of Renaissance and Reformation). Very early in *Richard II* we encounter the dilemma of resistance versus forbearance. John of Gaunt meets with the widow of Gloucester, while Woodstock, rising up as a specter (though from another play), leaves the impression that Richard was responsible for Woodstock's murder. Richard seems to have entered an undeclared war against his uncles, the six sons of Edward III – in comparison with whom and with the dashing promise of the Black Prince, his prematurely deceased father, the erring king is constantly portrayed as having fallen short. Lady Gloucester urges Gaunt to do something, to make some response to the death of his brother. "To safeguard thine own life, / The best way is to venge my Gloucester's death." Perhaps the recourse to personal vengeance casts a cold shadow over the enterprise, but Gaunt's attitude is one of forbearance: "God's is the quarrel." Richard is his anointed deputy, and as such can only be punished by divine vengeance, "for I may never lift / An angry arm against His minister" (I.iii.35–41).

But the counter-theory, the one that prevailed – was uttered by the Duke of York, after John of Gaunt had already on his death-bed denounced Richard's crimes, derelictions, and foppishness. His delinquencies are not cardinal but have amassed popular resentment. It is when in a reckless act he confiscates Bolingbroke's patrimony (against such an act Machiavelli had issued a warning) that York rises up in protest and predicts Richard's ultimate deposition. He has sawed off the limb on which his own legitimacy rests.

> Take Herford's [Bolingbroke's] rights away, and take from time
> His charters and his customary rights
> Let not tomorrow then ensue today;
> Be not thyself. For how art thou a king
> But by fair sequence and succession.   (II.i.195–9)

Richard's thoughtless lack of concern for his own tenure, born of an over-weening pride and fragile confidence, provides one justification for revolution. And this is demonstrated in the course of the play, as his removal is as much an act of abdication as it is of deposition. But as a true Elizabethan Shakespeare does not take revolution lightly, and ultimate vindication of Bolingbroke's actions can only come about through a long process of anxiety and expiation.

The crux of *Hamlet* depends upon the distinction between sin and vicious actions; the plot is moved by the young hero's failure to heed his dead father's counsel involving action and restraint. The first exhortation is "let not the royal bed of Denmark be a couch for luxury and damned incest," that is, remove the blot on the kingdom brought about by the foul machinations and degraded habits of Claudius. The second is "Taint not thy mind nor let thy soul contrive against thy mother aught – leave her to heaven and to those thorns that within her bosom lodge …" (1.v.81–7). The latter reminds Hamlet that God is responsible for the chastisement of sin; the former reminds him of his public responsibility to prevent foul actions from infecting the state. We have already been apprised that Claudius's ways involve more than unmannerly conduct. But Hamlet does "taint his mind" when his major preoccupation becomes his mother's sexual conduct; it is this which sets him back and prevents the enactment of his father's "dread command." Hamlet's extraordinary fixation on his mother's sexuality delays the execution of the first command. To such an extent are these two purposes crossed that in his mother's dressing room, where he rises in extracurricular fashion to berate her sexual activity, the second intervention of the ghost is required "to whet [his] almost blunted purpose" (3.iv.110–12). His distinction, perhaps tediously played out in Reformation theological tracts, is given living, dramatic justification by the genius of Shakespeare. It makes perfect sense that Hamlet has been summoned home from his studies at Wittenberg, that he advises Polonius of a grim theology: "Use every man after his desert, and who shall scape whipping" 2.ii.528–9), or that he advises where to find the body of Polonius – at a "convocation of politic worms" (4.iii.19–20; "your worm is your only emperor for diet"). Hamlet is framed by Shakespeare's vision of a university student of his day, whose background and that of the play (except for the purgatorial reference to the elder Hamlet's placement), is reflecting an intellectually alert, generalized form of Protestantism; as is the acuteness of the dilemma he faces.

Chapter Three

The Challenge of Ideas

The sixteenth century was the crucible of both immediate and long-term change. In fact, it represented in microcosm the battle lines as well as the continuing resolutions to the conflicts that would last into the eighteenth century and beyond. Huguenots in France went to war in order to achieve some religious freedoms, such as public houses of worship (granted in very limited circumstances by the various edicts culminating in the Edict of Nantes, 1598). William, Prince of Orange, clearly benefiting from Huguenot efforts, moved in his trajectory from Lutheran to Calvinist positions, thus epitomizing the radicalization of thought that occurred in the northern United Provinces. Where the methodical cruelty and calculated brutality of the Duke of Alba worked to intimidate and subdue the Southern provinces, they only stiffened the resistance in the North, an opposition that not only called for religious and civil freedom but also extended their demands for a change of government, a constitutional government rather than a monarchy. Remarkably enough, it was in the Netherlands that the first major split occurred between North and South, and this along confessional lines. But both in France and in the Netherlands there emerged a new type of political person, the *politique*, who sought to bring about an end to the strife, advocating peace and general toleration among all the parties, thus anticipating the coming course of enlightened thought, where elements of scepticism and tolerance entered into the mix.

The sections that follow will of course recall great events but interspersed with them will be the more pervasive concepts and principles that, whether they lead or follow, whether they are effects or causes, seem to be omnipresent. Each of these concepts was decisive in determining the North/South divide. These are cultural components, the issues and ideas that enter into all changes of belief, and that undergird the more evident responses. As already indicated, they are *Christian liberty, Christian* or *classical scepticism, tolerance*, and *time*. It is noteworthy that of the four, only Christian liberty is representative of moral value with origins in religious practice. The other three are not necessarily moral virtues but rather qualities of mind that are indicative of ways of being. They all represent codes of value. In their combined appeal and effectiveness they far surpass any "Protestant ethic" based upon Calvinist predestination. These are qualities that are easily carried over and recognized in human actions. History is not a free-floating balloon but is comprised of substances. These concepts are substantive values that open up areas within which people are free to develop their qualities. They are thus determinants that affect other issues such as the decline of empires, wars of religion, geography as causality or as a factor in receptivity. These are the lines drawn through this section. If the central problem and mark of difference between North and South was the willingness or unwillingness to accept or lead the way to change, then these four concepts are in the vanguard of the forces of change. Not only are they engines of change, they themselves undergo transformations. Once present, these cultural components have staying power.

Leading the way is Christian liberty, paramount in the early development of Luther and Erasmus, and their most important legacy. The other three figure as partners in their common enterprise, but given its primary role, Christian liberty serves as a majority partner. From the very beginning it was a blockbuster concept and in the course of its lengthy career underwent crucial transformations at the hands of powerful exponents. It may be considered the bright stream of Protestant belief. Theologically it offered to biblical humanists the possibility of accepting changes in canonical texts. As Jerome did in his time, so we in our time (they argue) have at our disposal the same right to bring correction. Moreover, liberty offered the individual the privilege of discernment in following or not following certain Church ordinances. Of the three great works that occupy the peak period of Luther's developing warfare with the Roman Curia, their agents, and their leader, Pope Leo X – *An Appeal to the Nobility of the German Nation as to the Amelioration of the State of Christendom, The Pagan Servitude of the Church* [Babylonian Captivity], and *The Freedom of a Christian* (all of 1520, a banner year) – the last is the fullest and most conciliatory.[1] In it Luther provides the means to approach the doctrinal matters of Scripture and to find a solid resting place for Christian belief in faith. Faith is the fundamental agency of salvation, a trust in the divine promise that although body and soul are corrupt and evil, their unworthiness has been absolved by virtue of Christ's sacrifice. It is thus through Christ that man knows himself to be free, free from the ceremonies and works that have been imposed by the Church and which do not contribute towards salvation. Once the soul is firm in its freedom and faith, none of the prohibitions and violations or injunctions can touch the inner person (54). "Therefore it is clear that works – whatever their character – cannot justify" (55–7).

Like a breath of fresh air, this upstanding notion of Christian liberty swept through the rules, ordinances, and provisions of the Church, even annulling the doctrine of "works" upon which so many of the sacraments depended. The belief that one can rest confident of salvation by observing the external directions of ecclesiastical protocol offered its comforts. But that would be to default on the freedom brought by Christ's sacrifice; one is no longer under the regime of the Law but rather that of the Spirit. For the reformers, in need of a more compelling conviction, the regime of the law only mires one more deeply into sinfulness, with no possible escape from its bondage. What a relief and joy Luther experienced when he underwent his reformational experience, discovering that his righteousness is not a product of his own doing, but rather bought by Christ's sacrifice, recognition of which can set him free. To a conscientious, hyper-scrupulous soul like Luther's, with an exacerbated sense of his own sinfulness, redemption by works, even good works, enmeshes him in an impossible task – he is engaged in a contest with himself. A severe, law-giving God is the manifestation of the quest for perfection in his own mind that made him prey to himself. This is an unwinnable contest because it is he himself who sets up the goals that defeat him. The quest for perfection, for fulfilment of the restrictions of the Law, only seems to send him further down into the ranks of the unholy. "If I lived and worked to all eternity, my conscience would never reach comfortable certainty as to how much it must do to satisfy God. Whatever work I had done there is always nagging doubt as to whether it pleased God or whether he required something more" (*The Bondage of the Will* 199). This poignant insight into his own psyche gives evidence of the remarkable sense of liberation attained by the realization that by himself there is no salvation (he was beating his fists at the wind, over many years, "to his great hurt") but that all depends upon the mercies of God bought by Christ's sacrifice. He is already saved. Observance of Church ordinances are not only ineffective as these conditions are man-made with little warrant from Scriptures, in fact they may be pernicious as only a true Christian spirit can lead to salvation.

Luther's scepticism about humanity's capacity to triumph over sin by means of personal resolutions is deeply layered. Commandments (Old Testament) are futile because we will always covet. Our failures – the failure of works – will only sink us more deeply into sin and desperation. Humankind is in need of a more radical uprooting, a more profound sense of its own inability, its worthlessness, and only then will it turn in readiness to rely on Christ (199). Without this faith no works can justify – whether accomplished by apostle or saint. The commandments are not fulfilled by works, there must be faith before works can fulfill the commandments. Not only is there a futility in commandments, there is also an inadequacy in works themselves. They do not seem to hold their value, are ephemeral, and cannot satisfy the whole person. Very few of the good things done come back to memory, and those that do have to be cajoled; but those dark stains and losses come back involuntarily, as it were, ambushing the unsuspecting soul. Put this way, one can see a close relationship between effectual practice of Freudian psychoanalysis (*mutatis mutandis*) and the faulty reliance on works – one cannot be saved by works, or by culture; rather one has a need for a personal faith, a true understanding of the self, an acquisition of faith, before one can meet the issues of one's life. Without this sense of inner being there is an incompleteness in works. This then is the way of true Christian liberty, which both delivers faith and is redeemed by faith. When possessed by this faith, humanity is free to choose or not to choose those things that are necessary or unnecessary for living and for salvation.

It is an easy thing to comprehend Luther's devaluing of ceremonials and works. For instance, he as well as Erasmus will maintain that it is preferable by far for a Christian to do neighbourly deeds, to take care of matters close to home, than to go on pilgrimages. But even such good deeds are not sufficient to provide salvation. It is for this reason *The Freedom of a Christian* is so concerned with the several varieties and meanings of works. Fundamental to Luther's spiritual economy is the dual nature of the person, made up of body and soul. While faith pertains to the upkeep of the soul, the soul must still reside in the body, and hence the active health of the body is important. The body must be disciplined to observe healthy practices and to avoid idleness. One does this not to secure righteousness but to be pleasing to God (67–8). Righteousness precedes practice.

There is a similar division of the spiritual economy when it comes to observable practices. One does not do or say all things at all times but instead follows a code of appropriateness. The difference lies between bodily matters and doctrinal. Mary did not need to be purified, but out of a freely offered love, and so as not to give offence or scandal, she consented. Paul agrees to circumcise Timothy so as not to alienate the Jews who did not yet understand the freedom of faith but when circumcision entered the debate over righteousness, whether such a "work" was essential for salvation, then he refused to allow the same for Titus (77).

It is in the context of the argument against the validity of works, that Luther will be challenged by Erasmus, when writing his diatribe on *The Freedom of the Will*. Luther would say that with this work Erasmus grabbed him by the throat. If a sense of being precedes works then it follows that good works do not make a good man, but a man does good works because he is good; evil works do not make a wicked man, but a man does evil works because he is evil (70). This amounts to a dangerous twist in Luther's moral universe. But of course it follows logically from his major premise. If works primarily make us good, then Erasmus and the Church are right and the entire ethical economy of Luther's reformational experience collapses (71–2). And here his prose reaches its most passionate concern, because he realizes the unacceptable consequences of admitting any primary status to works. Luther elevates the principle of appropriateness when dealing with non-Christians (where the Christian's faith is secure); in like manner, there is some complexity in his thought when it comes to works. Here even the faithful might fall. For this reason he must guard against abuses and beware the Pharisee within. Good works can puff us up, can give us a sense of superiority and thus increase our condemnation. On the other hand, there are those who will say, now that they are saved they have licence to act in any way they like and they have no need of works (67). Luther is suspicious of any determinations of principle that result in unseemly practices alien to true Christian belief. Here the scoffers are just as bad as the self-satisfied. The true antagonist seems to be glibness, the enemy of thoughtful pondering.

Just as the soul resides in the body, the Christian has neighbours, and thus as a natural emanation of righteousness we should devote every concern "to the service and benefit of others" (73–5). It follows that Christians should avoid tarnishing their faith by giving scandal. Luther's tone is vehement but his arguments are modulated. He does not join forces with those who attack for the sake of attacking, with those who push out emphatically against restrictions because they are restrictions. They are betrayed by superficiality and a want of spiritual understanding: "they want to show that they are free men and Christians only by finding fault with ceremonies, traditions and human laws; as if they were Christians because on stated days they do not fast or eat meat when others fast, or because they do not use accustomed prayers ..." (80). The extreme opposite are those who rely for their salvation solely on ceremonies, fasting, and certain prayers. Both are far from salvation, declares Luther, who is following a middle course adopted by Paul (81).

While this middling course might sound similar to that of Erasmus, they are still light years apart. It was Christian liberty that brought Luther and Erasmus together in their earlier careers and that opened up to each a world of freedom. In *Dualisms* I elaborated on this joint commitment. "The common thread, the one that finally unites Luther and Erasmus is the fundamental notion of Christian liberty, summarized in Jesus's own words that "the Sabbath is made for man, not man for the Sabbath" (32). This becomes an essential doctrine of reform extending to the larger Christian community: an adult laity, united in a common faith, is free to use its own discernment where many of the ordinances of the Church are concerned (11, 32, 74, 407n18). But this same Christian liberty becomes the point of contention as their presumed affinity only conceals the larger division between the two. In their great debate and public divergence, Luther, in detailing aberrations, excesses or erroneous applications always adheres to genuine principle, while Erasmus invokes Christian freedom itself. In a letter written from Basel in 1527, a chastened and subdued Erasmus now regrets his earlier advocacy of Christian liberty, "I am deeply grieved at having preached freedom of the spirit in earlier writing" (*Dualisms* 95). And where Luther condemns those who bristle at any restriction, and seem to be inveterate contrarians, Erasmus sees this same opposition to laws and regulations as endemic to Protestantism, a splintering effect that is its nearly fatal flaw: "at present some people are displeased by everything," and then he then goes on to add a crucial sentence, "And there is no end to this; there is always something to replace the old complaint" (*Selected Letters* 185).

There is a great conundrum in Luther's discussion of faith and works. It is a dilemma that returns us to some of the most complex moral and theological issues in the works of modern literature. Faith bestows a prior disposition to good deeds and lack of faith an inclination to evil deeds. But Luther's contention is even bolder: the deeds of a good man are good; the deeds of an evil man, evil. His evaluations derive from the "nature" of the person, not from the quality of the deeds. Yet, human wisdom is aware that a good man, a man of faith, can do evil works; and an evil man, a corrupt person, can perform good deeds. Such ambiguity seems to be lacking in Luther's moral universe. But there is a substantial sector of modern thought and letters which takes as its major object of investigation and concern this very tenet of Luther's belief. It is a remarkable fact that much of modern literature – and here I mean from Romantic literature onwards into Modernism – is driven to contest this very principle of Luther's thought. Its adherents would observe more complexity, more ambiguity in the conditions of existence. Their calling is for a greater intellectual justice. This is borne out in my study of the changeful worlds of Cain and Abel (*The Changes of Cain: Violence and the Lost Brother in Cain and Abel Literature*, 1991). Some indication of a more complex understanding is already offered in my discussion of Machiavelli, who introduced greater moral ambiguity when he exonerated Romulus for having slain his brother. His intention of serving the welfare of the state became apparent when he severely circumscribed his own powers. So, too, the good intentions of Bolingbroke in Shakespeare's second *Henriad* were manifest in his sense of guilt and contrition and his concern that Prince Hal be a monarch who recognizes his own subservience to the law.[2]

In their shared sense of the moral ambiguity of history and the dilemma of choice, Machiavelli and Shakespeare establish exempla of the Sacred Executioner who commits acts that are necessary for the foundation of the state or the beginning of a new regime. These "dark events" are questionable but their intentions are good, as evidenced by the self-imposed limitations on their power or by the ordeal of expiation they undergo.

Through much of modern literature this dilemma is removed from arguments pertaining to reasons of state and becomes more an emblem of life itself. The rich harvest of nineteenth-century works add to the Cain and Abel theme in its modern dress. This dramatic change in the moral structure of the theme transforms the relationship and character of the brothers. Now it is Abel who becomes the unmindful stay-at-home, while Cain assumes the burden of a complex consciousness. In Byron's *Cain,* which I shall employ as the epitome, Cain's ways are those of a just man – who calls on God to be the same – but who instead meets with the ancient mode of an Old Testament deity, who favours blood sacrifice. Offended that God should favour Abel's offering, he strikes his brother dead when Abel attempts to prevent Cain from desecrating the offending altar. The tough justice in Cain's character is apparent when he refuses to accept forgiveness but instead insists on his guilt.

This pattern of the pejoration of Abel and the moral ascent in character and sense of justice on Cain's part only increases in works of the nineteenth and twentieth centuries. It shows the Cain-Abel theme in its transformations to be the most potent in Western literature and its great appeal for this book is the increased moral dilemma it introduces into the formula that was Luther's – that good people do good deeds, and evil people evil deeds. A major strand of modern literature thus involves a serious second confrontation with the thought of Luther and this is clearly conveyed by the alterations occurring in the characters of Abel and of Cain. Abel might appear to be good but his virtue is wobbly, lacking. Cain does commit a crime but his motives are stalwart, his virtues of a different order, honest, forthright, misunderstood, because they are representing the changing values of the Enlightenment. The problem is brought to bear not upon the foundation of a state but rather on the changes of history itself. There remains a sternness in Cain's character as he insists upon his guilt but this only increases the moral quandary portrayed in the various accounts. Rather than denying Luther outright, the richness of the theme penetrates the perplexities of his thought when encountered in a different age by the renewed appeal of Erasmianism. The two stand ready to meet again but this time in a climate more favourable to Erasmus's irenic values. While Erasmus is crushed by Luther's vehement defence of assertion in their famous debate of 1525, his more modulated ethical plan receives its full endorsement when Erasmianism returns in the late seventeenth and early eighteenth centuries. The Enlightenment, which witnessed "the decline of Hell," the evanescence of original sin, the end of tragedy, among its more serious and attractive features, contributed greatly to the liberation of Cain. But as we shall see in discussing John Locke, its most fervent principle is that of a God who – if at all responsive to humane values – cannot endorse or perpetrate injustice. In this way the new intentions revealed by the changes in the Cain-Abel story help account for the advancement of the Northern appeal.

The sabbath is made for man not man for the sabbath, is Christ's own maxim of religious freedom that continued to resound through the coming centuries. It is invoked to establish the primacy of the inner man, the adult consciousness, who does not need others to tell him or her how to read or what to believe. Implicit in this argument is a tendency to go beyond theological matters, extending to political and civil liberties and a more basic freedom, that of thought.

In fact, religious liberty is invoked in major ways, from its regard for the inner person to its impositions of limitations on the powers of the State. It involves the responsibility to trust in one's own judgments. The exercise of judgment is the currency of adulthood. Not only was religious liberty equated to maturity, it rose to primacy of place in other ways as well. It and its companion propositions were decisive in intellectual warfare. The simple fact is that those countries which embraced these concepts emerged victorious in the great divide that confronted continental Europe, while those which rejected or diminished these propositions committed themselves to a decline in intellectual drive and to an unwelcomed but inevitable stagnation. Either version of Christian liberty – that of Erasmianism which underwent its own transformation, or that of Luther which staunchly held to fundamental principles – made essential contributions to civil liberties and to the defence of religious liberty against the encroachments of the State.

It is also true that those individuals who were fervently committed to Christian liberty and its later transformations (one can think of Milton or the Virginia intellectuals such as Jefferson and Madison) were those who had a particular abhorrence of the Inquisition. The two opposites existed on an axial polarity and could be considered in their growths as mutually offsetting. The Inquisition grew in reaction to the advance of religious liberties, and Christian liberty only intensified because of the increased power of the Inquisition. The former was guarded so jealously because of the latter: to infringe in any way on civil liberties or the separation of Church and State was to bring that much closer the threatening domination of the Inquisition. Their inherent conflict may have seemed to be that of distant opposites but it was very real and crucial for the growth of the various freedoms. This sensitivity to the encroachments of the Inquisition also points toward the later developments of civil liberties arising out of Christian liberty.

Chapter Four

Tolerance Twin to Incredulity

Scepticism enjoys a special relationship with tolerance. If one sees the world as a bundle of obscurities and contradictions, if one feels devoid of the Holy Spirit (as Erasmus lamented in searching moments of personal confession – see the letter to Marcus Laurinus of Feb. 1523, reprinted at length in *Dualisms* 93), one is less likely to take up arms or even to be adamant about truth. While on the other side, daemonic figures like Luther or Rousseau (who followed inner persuasions), could not tolerate scepticism. Rousseau could not imagine as tolerable a life lived in doubt. Yet scepticism did make its way into Rousseau's writings. It represented a procedural starting point for intellectual inquiry. What do I know after I have cleared the boards? What proposition can I derive that is indisputably solid and clear? Whatever one might think of the lived life of a sceptic, this is a feasible and resolute point of departure. *Que sais-je?*

Tolerance is a particularly skittish concept. No sooner does one enter into the domain of tolerance than one discovers its limitations in practice. States founded on religious freedom, or dedicated to that principle, soon find themselves obliged, if only out of self-preservation, to limit the concept in practice. The victorious radical Calvinists of the northern provinces of the Netherlands may allow liberty of conscience to Catholics, Jews, and ... Lutherans, but not its public practice. Pierre Bayle's recriminations against his Protestant brethren stand out as a serious warning against this prohibition. But founders and protectors of statehood, those who waged war and struggled to establish a state, will always be concerned to protect and preserve their achievement. Additional limitations, if not deficiencies, in the theory and practice of tolerance will be discussed below in chapter 9.

Christian liberty and tolerance are two major tributaries that enter into the formation of the Northern divide. Neither found support among the antagonists of the South, whose powers, tested by "negative proofing," only harmed themselves by their failure to do justice to these principles. The validity of these concepts is demonstrated by the negation of those who fought their adoption. By their failures you shall know them. While Christian liberty owed its political wedge to the pioneering thought of Luther and Erasmus, tolerance had a long and tangled history, and can display a complex nature. Tolerance, like the chameleon, can change colours, a feature which may account somewhat for its tepid historical assessment.

Similar to that of scepticism, its lineage predates the sixteenth century. As Peretó Rivas has shown in his collection of essays, *Tolerancia: Teoria y práctica en la Edad Media*, it made an early appearance in the thought of one of the Greek fathers of the Church, Gregory of Nyssa – thought that carried far into the future. We are made in the image of God and should therefore show forbearance and compassion towards our brothers; we are all children of God, hence equality should reign between man and wife, and between men to the exclusion of slavery (Francesco Harriet, in Peretó Rivas 14).

The classical world with its plethora of gods and goddesses could easily absorb any variety of opinions and beliefs (Rome even had a god for the sewers, Cloacina, and one for manure, Sterculinus). This world also tended to value powers or unmistakable presences. "As long as Christians, like members of other religions, carried out their secular duties, the State had no right to interfere with the consciences of individual Christians" (Kamen, *Toleration* 9). Both by the doctrine of appropriateness and Christ's sense of the two separate kingdoms, where one renders to Caesar those things that are Caesar's and to God, those that are God's (Matthew 22:21), Christians could very well have been accepted within Roman culture. But they ran into difficulties when they opposed the traditional gods and customs of Roman societies, the reliance on oracles, and the animal sacrifices, but most importantly when they elevated a mere human, and a contemporary at that, to the godhead. For such divinization, the Romans found more to fault in the apostles than in Christ.

From the Middle Ages come brief, quotable phrases to express the exclusive dominance of the Church, its suppression of heretical beliefs, and its "tough love" against tolerance: "What death is worse for the soul than the liberty to err?" "The church persecutes out of love, the ungodly out of cruelty." "The Church provides the one path alone ..."[1] Thus the first and abiding encounter of tolerance is with intolerance. But such rigidity was always more supple than was once generally thought. There existed a division between theory and practice (as the essays collected by Peretó Rivas show), because some practices which had not been granted official approval were permitted for reasons of social utility. Brothels, usury, and the useful skills of some minorities fell within this allowance. The phrase, tolerance, was slowly sliding over from its original designation, meaning to endure a sickness or other misfortune with patience and fortitude, to the secondary meaning of granting some allowance towards another person or cause. *Ecclesia non approbat sed permittit.* Social utility was granted a limited use permit but we are still far from the early modern and modern uses of the term.

Tolerance in its more modern dress as a controversial concept had its origins in the sixteenth and seventeenth centuries among the Huguenots and the revolutionary thinkers of the United Provinces. Tolerance differs sharply from Christian liberty by virtue of its alliance with scepticism, whether Christian or simply classical. From the Reformation on, its proponents and its opponents occupy positions made familiar by the debate between Erasmus and Luther, Luther an ardent advocate of assertion when it comes to Christian principles, and Erasmus admitting a strong inclination towards scepticism but for the disapproval of the Church.

> "And I take so little pleasure in assertion that I would gladly seek refuge in skepticism whenever this is allowed by the inviolate authority of Holy Scripture and the Church's decrees; to these decrees I fully submit my judgment in all things, whether I fully understand what the Church commands or not." (*Dualisms* 89)

This archly composed, highly qualified statement manages to provoke a triple explosion in Luther. A few paragraphs after quoting Erasmus he intones, "The Holy Spirit is no sceptic." He calls Erasmus Protean in character, unwilling to be pinned down. Erasmus is guilty of forswearing his prior commitment to Christian liberty. Instead, he is willing to finally subject their liberty in uncritical fashion to the decrees of men. "Where does the Scripture of God impose this on us?" Luther asks. Erasmus can thus play the even-handed mediator who tries to weigh equitably several viewpoints (the classical meaning of diatribe, by which Erasmus refers to this work), with the implication being that they are finally arguing about things that are pointless (90). The opposing energies and issues of this powerful debate will be a constant in the ages to come, where Christian liberty will be transformed into civil liberty, and Erasmian scepticism will shed its ambivalences and only grow in argumentative appeal.

We now turn back to Erasmus, whose thought and character are always present, and who best represents the alliance between scepticism and tolerance. Erika Rummel presents a full and cogent argument for Erasmus's Christian scepticism, and Erasmus is the first of the "moderns" invoked in Richard Popkin's classic study, *The History of Scepticism from Erasmus to Spinoza*. A generous dose of Christian scepticism colours Erasmus's view of the world and the positions he adopts. The obscurity clouding all things, except simple articles of faith, should instill a modesty in argumentation, a lack of dogmatism, and certainly remove most causes for war. We have already called attention to the New Testament justification for scepticism in the rhetorical approaches of Peter, Paul, and even Jesus. They do not say all things at all times; expediency is a key note, appropriateness as to time, to audience, and to message. Moreover, as there is such obscurity in human affairs, how much more is there in divine matters. In that crucial letter to Marcus Laurinus in 1523 – as well as in his memorable debate with Luther – Erasmus announces his own way of finding peace and consensus. The impasse of scepticism returns him to the bosom of the Church and to the wisdom handed down through generations. As a reverential humanist he bows before the ages. Furthermore, in matters of dispute, after the original outburst and flashes of argumentative anger, the wear of war and time itself will bring reconciliation. A recurrent travel companion of tolerance is time, which manages to take the edge off the sharpness of debate, which wears down opposition, and where changes, surprises, and mollification temper the heat of dispute. And if it does not reduce the heat, at last it can dissipate the smoke. These working effects of scepticism will increase and be added to in its later developments.

That tolerance has such an alliance with scepticism is not always in its favour. All positions can become mere matters of opinion, and opinion, like taste, *non est disputandem*. Erasmus's scepticism can lead to a tendency towards conciliation that is a product of passivity and other failures of personality. An intellectual sluggishness takes hold that blurs lines of debate. One will make note how this middling, conciliatory position differs from Milton's more burning, explosive sense of scepticism, which leads to forthright action in the present. Milton was a poet, Protestantism's native son, unlike Erasmus who was in his time a middle-man soon to be crushed by the confessionalists from either side. To later generations, particularly those of Voltaire and Rousseau, Erasmian scepticism found its way back as an intellectual counter; in fact, for both thinkers it serves as an intellectual starting-point and the basis of their mutual suspicion of great systems of thought.

Once again Erasmus is an initiating figure, but one whose influence is more diffuse. Although Erasmus never wrote a full treatise on tolerance, his works exude it. His character, emotional temperament, his opposition to zealotry, dogmatism, and fanaticism, his devotion to concord and peaceful communion, as W.K. Ferguson argues when piecing together Erasmus's fugitive statements, form the essence of tolerance ("Attitudes of Erasmus towards Tolerance"). Despite religious differences, which are usually matters of opinion, people ought to be able to live together as brothers. There are more essential articles of faith that unite Catholic and Lutheran than there are reasons for division (see the Colloquy, "The Examination Concerning Faith").[2] To Erasmus's forgiving mind, so aware of error in humans and obscurity in things both religious and secular, even heresy should be limited to seditious propositions before drawing down the wrath of the State. He believes that the Turk could more readily be won over by examples of Christian love than by expressions of hostility. The example of Erasmus, his character, and his diverse and wide-ranging writings, re-emerge through subterranean currents as Erasmianism and count for much in the four concepts that this volume emphasizes. We recognize its presence in his followers.

Chapter Five

The Paradox of Time and the Moderns

Just as tolerance and scepticism share a historically joined relationship, so do Christian liberty and time. They can be brought into a closer affiliation because each was a powerful concept that enjoyed special status within Protestantism. Both were strongly directed towards the future and both enjoyed a complexity or ambiguity that tended to unseat the very principles from which they stemmed. A new sense of time, dramatic and intense, gained added force with the coming of Protestantism, but that was because the actuality of time in the Renaissance had features quite congenial to Protestantism. It required that each individual take the reins of his or her life and get a better grip on an existence that is fraught with peril. Mastery of time appealed to the Protestant temper and thus to the rising Northern states as well. But in the twentieth century it was this very tight hold on life that contributed to the dissolution and distress from which the first sprouts of literary modernism began to emerge. There is a reason why literary modernism found its origins in Northern Europe: it was there that the Renaissance sense of time had its fullest development (despite starting as it did in the Italian 'Trecento) and its breaking-point.

Time in the Renaissance has many faces and many purposes. One aspect, however, is clear: like inches, feet, yards, it is a measure of reality. We need it to know when we are where we are, or at what time we will be where we want to be. But unlike other forms of measurement, it has human and emotional implications. It is brought to birth in two ways in the early years of the fourteenth century in Italy: it is the era when the growing and enterprising Italian cities advertised their prosperity with the first mechanical clocks posted high in public view, and simultaneously, time entered the first stirrings of the renascent literature as an intensely dramatic force.

Yet, paradoxically, time is not an idea, or, if so, it is a very elusive one. Hence the Augustinian dilemma: in his own mind, he seems to know what time is, but when asked to explain its nature he is baffled. Time is the only element that is not what it is. Weighty, it is weightless. Pointed, it is pointless. Inducing death, it is deathless. Invisible, it requires the infusion of other forces to make itself discernible, to materialize: we only see it when the trees bend with age, or wattles appear on the neck under the chin. It may be described at second hand or illustrated by images. It is the ultimate "socialized" theme and thus ripe and ready to incorporate other working ideas. In the Renaissance time acquires an argument. It takes on the qualities of a fickle monster that devours where at first it fostered. But it is part of the active energy of the Renaissance that response can be made, in fact is called for. Primarily this occurs in two ways: either by children or by fame, progeny or accomplishment, "perfection of the life or of the works," in Yeats's memorable epigram.[1] And thus we start with a tripartite manifest: the configurations of time as an agent of a destructive reality, and the means available to humankind to seek out some recourse against a marauding brigand.

One of the major indicators of what Cassirer has termed the "originality" of the Renaissance may be found in this new sense of time.[2] Indeed, this grasp of time has been called the essential dynamic of the West. Everything it touches moves. Even the imaginative reception of time has altered. One no longer lies quiescent in the hands of God, or reclines on one's adobe porch watching the sun set in the West, or endures helplessly the ravages of Nature. Time has acquired a destructive arsenal. Faced with this predator, one can no longer sit passively but is obliged to make vigorous response. Throughout the Renaissance these components form the argument of time. The unheeding must be alerted to their faulty sense of invulnerability and accordingly must take appropriate measures. Prudence is called for, a new realism; a broad movement is underway where people are urged to make provision; in some dramatic works, indeed in Shakespeare's second tetralogy, this is portrayed as a movement from the sacramental to the secular, from the God-supported majesty of *Richard II* to the hard scramble and necessity of mastering time in the dramas that follow. Overwhelmingly in those sectors of Europe where the Renaissance has taken hold, one finds advocates of an active response to time by either of the two rejoinders – children and fame – that promote the continuity of house and home, of self and name. One must avoid the terrible lament of Richard II that resounds for all to hear: "I wasted time and now doth time waste me ..." (*Richard II* V.v.49). And he is supplanted, replaced, confronting only spoiled possibilities, with no name or children, no addition; he has squandered his patrimony, a wastrel whose lamentations only serve to mark the time of Henry IV's victory.

The shared assumptions between Protestantism and the new, dramatically compelling sense of time have made for valuable exchanges among leading historians of economic development (Hobsbawm, *The Age of Capital* 263). Most of these arguments will be presented in chapter 10 of this volume; here I will simply follow the words of David Landes, who in *The Wealth and Poverty of Nations*, while allowing many of the charges made against Max Weber's contested thesis, nevertheless finally agrees with Weber, as he addresses both theoretical and empirical levels. "In manufacturing centers ... in France and Western Germany Protestants were typically the employers, Catholics the employed." The same was true in Switzerland, where as early as the mid-eighteenth century both Voltaire and Rousseau could distinguish between Protestant and Catholic cantons by their signs of prosperity and diligent cultivation. Landes considers this new sense of time to be an essential ingredient of the active Protestant societies (*Revolution in Time* 92–3).[3] Technically, Protestants were the great clock-makers, as well; witness the St Gervais section of Geneva where Rousseau grew up. But even in Catholic countries (France and Bavaria) clockmakers were Protestants (*Wealth and Poverty* 178). In his *Idées Républicaines* Voltaire counts the number of idle feast days in the Catholic calendar and concludes they amounted to as much as one month of non-productivity out of the year.[4]

Landes supports Max Weber's thesis that Protestantism had provided an "ethos" for economic advancement; a new type of man – "rational, ordered, diligent, productive" – brought recognized standards of judgment. Allowing for all the exceptions, in Northern Europe from the sixteenth to eighteenth centuries, religion encouraged the growth in numbers of a personality type that had been exceptional and adventitious before, and this type created a new economy (a new mode of production) that we know as "(industrial) capitalism" (178–9). Literacy among Protestants became more valued and this led to an increased time-consciousness and a wider gulf between Catholics and Protestants. Landes's evidence is the spread of time pieces, where "their diffusion to rural areas was far more advanced in Britain and in Holland than in Catholic countries" (178). Such a tell-tale sign of the reversal of values can thus be figured, when the prime agent of urbanization takes possession of what should have been the rural strong hold of resistance to such advances.

But there is another dimension of time that brings into contention two great periods – the Renaissance and Modernism – and for that very reason is discussed here. One is a period made up of movements and the other is a movement that becomes a period. Despite its more abbreviated (or accelerated) duration, Modernism engages with the Renaissance in that each brought forth separate revolutions in time. In the Renaissance we witnessed a renewed faith in progeny and fame, as proper responses to the depredations of Time. Girding these emergent values was a larger faith in continuity itself. Time forwards and time backwards can reach as far into the future as Utopia and as far away into the past as the Golden Age. These mythic projections enjoyed a joint revival in the Renaissance. Together they rested on an even greater faith and that was in the validation of human action. Despite all the feelings of guilt and depression, despite all the complexities of motive and emotion, human action could be vindicated.

In a modest revision of the counterbalances to Time as defined by the Renaissance, modernists reconfigured "children and fame" into "family and work."[5] But even with this subtle revision there is a discernible contraction in how far one's influence or life extends. We act for a moment or for a day. T.S. Eliot can give an extreme expression to such scepticism (in fact, his poetry might be considered "poetry at the extreme") when he decries the assurances bestowed by experience: "… every moment is a new and shocking / Valuation of all we have been."[6] Yeats's epigram tells the story as one of a generation's intellectual devolution:

Shakespearean fish swam the sea, far away from land;
Romantic fish swam in nets coming to the hand.
What are all those fish that lie gasping on the strand?   (236)

While Modernists may not exhibit energy and dynamism – the qualities by which Cassirer characterizes the Renaissance – they still have virtues of their own. Theirs is the struggle to keep to a chosen path, to become figures of a free-standing consciousness. Their travail comes from the fact that their struggle is directed against the time-world that the Renaissance created. Two great revolutions meet in conflict: the one established, solidified, in fact, largely responsible for the emergence of the North; the other in need of shedding this inheritance, of avoiding entrapment, of establishing a new style with new values, deliberately set in opposition to the values ushered in by the Renaissance.

This confrontation may be explained by a change in the Renaissance ethic, by what we have called "the paradox of time."[7] In his classic essay on Goethe and Tolstoy (a prelude to his monumental novel *Der Zauberberg*), Thomas Mann points up the issues succinctly. Unlike his Renaissance forefathers who signalled the beginning of a new time, he admits its coming to an end, the end of the bourgeois, humanistic, liberal epoch, which was born at the Renaissance and came to power with the French Revolution. This raises the question "whether the Mediterranean, classic, humanistic tradition is commensurate with humanity ... or whether it is only the intellectual expression and appanage of the bourgeois liberal epoch and destined to end with it."[8] Hugh Grady in his *The Modernist Shakespeare* performs a service when he describes the "shift" in the time worlds of the Renaissance and Modernism (98–102). The noose was tightening. One senses it in the narrowness of consciousness that confines Prufrock, in the clenched fists of Gustav von Aschenbach and in the open susceptibility of the young engineer Hans Castorp to the siren song of the magic mountain. Saddled with these burdens, one grows tired of the repetitive sheet music and the empty rhetoric of the humanist revivalist Settembrini.

Like Erasmus and Luther, modernists were part of a youthful, generational revolt. Like them, they had enemies to confront and values to assert. But here the similarities end. As mentioned previously, Erasmus and Luther were blessed with gifts – opponents whom they were to demote and dismiss, and possibilities arising from their own creative energies and positive programs. The world they upended was a world at odds with itself and forgetful of its purposes. Modernists entered history by entirely different doors; the variance between their two situations was enormous. The modernists were obliged to encounter not a world of superstitious remnants or even individual or corporate venalities, but a rational world order, an easily derived, solidly based culture of known certainties, as straightforward as $2 + 2 = 4$; a constructive world filled with the marvels of science and medicine, of automobiles, sky-scrapers, telephones, radios, and forward forever. This world was primarily of the North, mainly Protestant, successful, and optimistic. The accompanying world view is grossly satirized in Dickens's Gradgrind from *Hard Times*, who is mindful only of facts, and "there's an end to it." Yeats gives more gentle expression to the reality he is seeking to alter, "O what fine thoughts we had because we thought / That the worst rogues and rascals had died out" (Yeats 203). "Nineteen Nineteen," the title year of Yeats's poem that was supposed to reap the harvest of peace, only served to reveal deeper turmoil and unrest, and the anticipation of harsher things to come. The rule of nations was not working out and all the assumptions, the hopes, and even triumphs of the newly won world order were crumbling before their very eyes in Europe and in the US.

What birthed this new dissident movement? What was it that caused their unrest? The horrors committed along the highways evoked in Yeats's poem were reason enough, but there was a fundamental problem with the very metaphysics of time that had developed from the Renaissance, a problem that affected both style and substance. The circumscribed bourgeois world was not wrong; it was incomplete, dull, and limited to the point of exasperation. By its very rational nature, it observed the proprieties but more as though they were protocols which they were compelled to observe than articles of faith they were eager to embrace. Just as Abel experienced depreciation in the changes to the brotherhood to which he had belonged, so the orderly bourgeois world underwent its own transformations. The Holy Spirit that counted so much for Luther and even the early Erasmus had been undone. The young modernists encountered and engaged a hypertrophied world suffering from the effects of the Renaissance time-plan, and a world revealing the changes that the Reformation had also undergone – a loss of energy and purpose. Jean-Paul Sartre, a second-generation Modernist, enshrined for all time the smugness that had overtaken Lutheranism when he quotes with relish in the autobiographical *Les Mots* his grandfather's fatuous utterance, "My children, how nice it is when there is nothing for which one can reproach oneself" (*Dualisms* 387). The Modernist revolt operates thus on more than one front. The biggest change that I could have brought to *Mapping Literary Modernism* would have been to create greater room for the Reformation, it too becoming in time an establishment that had lost its fervor.

What had gone wrong with the Western pace of time? This is the general question that almost all new movements ask, only now it is directed against the epoch that had discovered (or rediscovered) the crucial value of time. Clearly some revulsion and recoil had occurred. It has to do with the complex nature of the Renaissance time-world and its more simplified articulation in the nineteenth century. There were two aspects to the Renaissance discovery of time. One was electrifying, exciting, expansive, and innovative, what Cassirer meant when he referred to that period's "dynamism," or what Petrarch meant when he spoke of a fundamental contest with Time: "ingentibus animis nichil breve optabile est (to those who have greatness of soul nothing brief is worthy)" There was wind in the sails and lift in the stride. But such energy needed to be controlled, and regulated. The second aspect reveals a disciplined response to time. "Everything consists in the ordered disposition of time" (*Renaissance Discovery of Time* 496).

From Petrarch forward, we find reference to such techniques as doubling-up (multitasking?) where two things were done simultaneously, given the preciousness of time. It was left to the unfettered Gallic spirit of Montaigne to bring the exhortations to a destined end, when he complained, "Next they'll have us shitting on the run." Here scatology is revealing: it is not by extension but by concentration, Montaigne means, that one plumbs the depths of things. Things acquire texture and density by the degree of intense focus to which they are subject. Still, in the newly developing consciousness, Time was not to be wasted. As a great discovery with metaphysical and cosmic reverberations, time led also to practical decisions and mundane consequences. It needed an ethic to provide ballast for its metaphysic. From Petrarch to Erasmus and Rabelais, and among a host of humanists coming between and after, it acquired a program of studies, a schedule, the newly devised *emploi du temps*. Clocks were to be provided for libraries, effectively encouraging people to read against time rather than engage in true reading which, like fishing or gaming, is forgetful of time.

These two impulses, however well-coordinated, were actually opposite in nature. In the course of events the impetus to regulate and control took precedence over the action of discovery. And this is where the paradox occurs. When the predictive, controlling aspect of time triumphed so thoroughly and one-sidedly it paradoxically produced its opposite effect – the triumph of space. E.M. Cioran's *La chute dans le temps* is actually about the fall out of time. Just as humankind has fallen out of eternity, so it can fall out of time. If all times become alike then they no longer exist as changeful succession but as sameness. History itself is defeated, or comes to naught. Stasis, and want of forward motion or the energy to move forward take over. Unlike what should happen with succession, one meets with repetition ("the same as new," quips Joyce). One is bogged down, Cioran writes, "in inertia, in dreariness, in the absolute of stagnation" (192).

Among the medieval monks it was known as *acedia*, or sloth; in Renaissance thought, it was described as "melancholia," and in modern, post-scientific thought as "ennui." For some it was the loss of belief in the right functioning of a moral universe; but for others it was a feeling of sheer absence – no one is there to pick up the phone. Robert Frost's memorable poem "Acquainted with the Night" (255) brings an apparently abandoned lover or one mourning a loss to a city walk where nothing intervenes to comfort his sense of forlornness. His aimless motion takes him beyond the farthest city light. The further example of this loss of an answering or forgiving voice exists at an "unearthly height" – the luminous light of the clock that "proclaimed the time was neither wrong nor right." He stands alone without traditional supports; he sought a world of vindication but instead finds one of withdrawal, a world that is neutral. But neutrality where one expected endorsement is a negative vote. The presence of Frost, normally assumed to be comforting, is at times not that far from the Heideggerian sense of being "thrown" into existence; here he is thrown *out* of life's ways. The collapse of humanism that Mann described is here given poetic representation.

In Ingmar Bergman's *Wild Strawberries* (1957) a distinguished medical researcher, Isak Borg, at the age of 77 is about to receive an honorary degree for his work. But he dreams of walking down an emptied street in an abandoned section of the city with the solitary presence of a blank face of a public clock that has no hands. In the course of the film he is afflicted by painful recollections of his past life, which had been one-sidedly devoted to scientific labour. In two such crucial episodes men who have their way with women intervene to take away his idealized relationship with a betrothed, and later with his wife. The men are worldly wise and the women, despite protestations that are more formalities than real, yield. He had chosen a path for perhaps the wrong reasons and now was reaping the effects, conscious of a sense of emptiness. These are the events, with their hold on his memory, that render him devoted to science where there are no such infidelities. He never as a youth tasted wild strawberries. The clock in Frost's poem highlights his keen sense of personal injury while the clock (and later watch) that has no hands reveals the bitter disappointments of Borg's life and a world where time has literally become empty space. We are reminded of Thomas Mann's theme of the Protestant North, of a life of personal sacrifice that has come to an abyss of regret over love both neglected and betrayed. One is caught in a cycle of nothingness, of psychic standstill represented by the time-pieces which lend no support. Time is a dead issue, as the clocks emptied of their contents indicate. They have fallen out of time. Thus even the very triumphal presence of time's indicator, the hands marking hours and minutes, has turned into its opposite, space.

A third example, even bleaker and more distressful, conveying the more complex understanding of the changing views of time in literary modernism, is found in an earlier poem by T.S. Eliot, *"Rhapsody on a Windy Night"* (see also n6 this chapter). If Prufrock takes us on a journey, it is through space; *Rhapsody* takes us on a journey through time. Five of the six stanzas are introduced by declarations of the time, usually on the half-hour, except, that is, for the final indication of the time as four a.m. by the street lamp that has probably served as the source of the other temporal indications. And as in *Prufrock* what is shown, what is witnessed, what is revealed is the collapse of the welcoming world of humanism (to employ the strategy that Thomas Mann traced above). The world experience is one of alienation, and the aesthetic that of the opposite of empathy, or, as Wilhlem Worringer put it, as *entfremdung*. The poem brilliantly conveys the aspects of cultural alienation: we observe the discards of a culture, experience primitive regression, distortion of the human image, and are exposed to a concentration on the subterranean, cellular undersides of existence, a world turned inside out. What we witness and even find enticing is the lurid life of an underworld. The visitation is courtesy of the agonist, who like Prufrock is an emotional participant in what he sees. At least he is drawn to it. Like Aschenbach in *Death in Venice*, his intense and ulterior desire is to be united with the loathsome objects and the experiences they imply. Prufrock gives expression to this wish for a union with the inhuman: "I should have been a pair of ragged claws / Scuttling across the floors of silent seas."

The different tenor of the last stanza of *Rhapsody* helps us to understand the curious turn of much modern art and literature, why this "dehumanization" should be one part of modernist artistic expression, and how it brings the parts of the poem together as an emotional whole, whereas the other stanzas seem to expand on a theme, summarized as what underlies the bare bones of existence. Making it clear that it is the street lamp that is showing the time, the last stanza begins, "The lamp said, / four o'clock." In stanzas 1, 2, 4, 5, the street lamp telling the time is also the conductor of what is seen, of the vistas of subhuman existence. But in the last stanza, there is no vision of depravity, there is, rather, a return to the vestiges of an ordinary life, which is, in fact, the problem as it is this habitual existence that constitutes "the last twist of the knife." At the dissolution of memory, with "all its clear relations / its division its precisions," we are rendered vulnerable to the street scenes of an accommodating underworld. The last stanza jerks us back to a delimited, mechanical, robotic life. Stylistically, there are pronounced differences between the two parts. While descriptions in the other stanzas are at least developed and quite graphic, involving all the senses, including that of smell (for example, in the penultimate stanza's concluding eleven lines, the olfactory sense, the most primitive of our receptors is referred to five times), the last stanza only includes one adjective attached to a noun: "A little lamp." Its style is telegraphic (as is that of Camus in the first part of *The Stranger*). There are other even more important differences. It is in this stanza that Memory, as the basic repository of mechanical reactions, returns. But this is a Memory that issues commands (such as "Mount"), and lays out an *emploi du temps*. But what he orders is what has already taken place, the transcript of the agonist's ordinary days and ways. The organized life takes hold, but it is one that is reduced to the barest elements of existence. But this reduction of life's plan is given in primer clauses, even blunt commands: "The bed is open, the tooth brush hangs on the wall / Put your shoes at the door, sleep. Prepare for life." His life is being given over to the mechanical. How is he to be prepared for life by this banal mundanity, or better yet, for what kind of life? The kind that finds itself so vulnerable to being engrossed by the obscene. This world of mechanical ordering is what enacts the last twist of the knife. The focus of what we have just seen has already produced a sort of self-immolation, the loss of his being in the sordid images cast up by naked existence. But those episodes are joined by this other hand on the knife, that of his spectacularly boring routinized existence, breeding a hyper self-consciousness that is an accomplice to the previous incursions into a void. The poem is remarkable, in that, with a great degree of exactness, it reproduces the humdrum paradox of time, where the regularity of scheduled activity breaks out into unconscious revolt, stimulated by the need for the profane if not the obscene, the disorderly. Hell may be preferable to nothingness but in this stanza nothingness is on a par with, if not creative of, Hell. This is the start of Eliot's "poetry at the extreme"; in the larger intellectual world, the banal routinization of existence prompted the modernists to seek out other bases for living. Some characteristics of poetry among the moderns will undergo variations depending upon the artist or writer; but one purpose remains, to dramatically present *in artistic form*, as a protest against the standardization of social life, the subterranean ordures of existence. It is one of the first principles of modern art (though not the only one).

This is one of the driving forces of Modernism. Its grand encounter with the Renaissance – at least where time is the concern – reveals a world without tomorrow, a motorcade come to a halt. The energy of the Renaissance – appropriated by northern Protestantism – has been stalled, abated, and in some cases perverted. But the result is clear: the victory of the predictive over the innovative, once held together in a delicate balance, has produced the triumph of space, which has itself become immobilized, lacking in forward movement.

These four topics (with scepticism and tolerance still to be discussed more fully) are valid intellectual barometers of the great *differences* intruding between North and South. These are real points of contest and factors of change. Their validity is shown in their influence on the nature of governments and the manners and mores of society (Voltaire's criteria). They are justified by what I term "negative proofing." These are not ships passing in the night; their advocates meet in close intellectual combat. This is an ideological civil war; they each knew whereof they disputed. Unlike alien cultures fighting over different ideals and values, these opposing forces meet on an intellectual battlefield to determine acceptance or rejection of these concepts. The validity of these concepts – the substance of their values – is shown by the fact that those countries that rejected them are sinking in their own misfortunes. Since these four propositions are concepts, they are there to be adopted or rejected. Conflict is not over a material object, a piece of pie, where your enemy's share diminished yours. Rather, in theory, there can be no winners and losers, but "blessed winners all." In their own free fall the Southern countries chose to despise these advanced concepts and thus helped to sink their own boats. In this way these concepts acquire substance and their opposition or suppression must have negative results. This is what I mean by negative proofing. The very features that had become so prominent in the North, when absent, help account for the decline of the South.

The concepts whose transformations I follow, the explosion of new ideas with new methods are palpably present in the thought and practices of the North, but their various manifestations were reviled with comparable energy in the countries and voices representing the South. Tolerance was deemed "hellish," and Clement VIII reviled the Edict of Nantes and its concession to liberty of conscience as "the worst thing in the world." And so it happened: the refusal to accept the challenges of well supported new ideas and fundamental changes meant the relegation of the South to enclosed and restricted confines, the closing of books and the shutting down of borders, and ultimately, intellectual stagnation. One might attribute this regression to a malaise, a sclerosis, but in fact it was in large part due to the failure to accept these new propositions. This adds some real meat to Hegel's dictum in *The Philosophy of History* that the southern Catholic countries failed to encompass the Spirit of the Age (419).

Quite simply, the presence or the absence of these major concepts forms the "mechanisms" and energies of change or the equally strong pressures of decline. In negative proofing the divided parties are separated by the very factors that joined them and the value of the concepts is ascertained by the failure of the contestants who devalued these propositions. The very same ideas identifiable with the emergence of the North were available to the South but were confronted and rejected by the losers in this great combat. This is a debate, a dualism if you will, founded on the same principles. This means that parties were equally free to adopt means of success, but some did not, or could not. This was not a fatalistic or determined outcome, but rather the outcome of a bitter clash between rival powers. Nor was the outcome immediately apparent, rather it took decades of continuous dispute before the dust had settled. Even John Stuart Mill in his *On Liberty* can engage in "what if" speculation to indicate the constant threat represented by opposing forces.[9] What if Queen Mary had lived and Elizabeth had died? Such counterfactual ideations are merely intriguing but do suggest how easily – in the short run – the equation could have been altered or the balance tipped in a different direction (97).

These four concepts bring out with much greater clarity and detail the complex issues at stake. They are indicators of a culture's dynamism, of its readiness to confront in a resolute way the problems it faces. They all had their common origins or periods of intensified awareness (as with tolerance and time) in the epoch of the Reformation; they all underwent the general transformation from their religious origins to modes of secularization. In their forward advancement and appeal they served to separate decisively the Protestant camps and their allegiance from the characteristic beliefs of the South. It was over these concepts that disputes arose; they were the standards and banners of battle. In them we can see into the heart of the debate and find the reasons for divergence. They do not derive from some "rhetorical unconscious" (see below, chapter 10); they are consciously adopted and held positions, points of fervent awareness.

Chapter Six

Characters and Causality

The origin of the North/South divide in the Reformation is a double-edged sword. One edge opened the way to the proliferation of sects and the fierce hostilities among them and between the established nation states and the newly formed and tenacious minority groupings within the state. But there is another side to this sharpened weapon and that is the creative response that grew out of the Reformation and knew no stopping only constant transformation and increased appeal. These are two sides to the same sword. Of the many possibilities offered to Reformers this study emphasizes the four concepts. Their growing appeal and their transformations will mainly be found in the countries of northern Europe. That these countries were primarily Protestant suggests not only reasons for reception of these principles but that their adoption was causative and helped to create the capabilities that brought these countries to the forefront of European life and thought. Each of these principles in their separate or combined ways will be present and active in the emergence of the North.

The South, by refusing out of fear to permit freedom of belief and conscience, blocked its own way forward. The streams of dissident exiles and émigrés were, within certain limits, welcomed in the Northern countries. It is certainly true in part that the North developed because it accepted diligent individuals who had found themselves threatened in the South by the Inquisition in Spain and the post-Tridentine world in Italy. As the South became the stronghold of rejection, the North became a providential habitat for developing thought and industry.

This chapter leads into a discussion of causality, of the causes that occur in response to character, that is, causality on the smaller scale, but also of the causality that determines character or that is believed to do so. This is causality in the broader sense, that of geography and climatic conditions. These conditions are invoked as a means of explaining the hegemony of the North, but such an explanation could also not occur before that precedence became apparent.

But when did the North/South divide begin to enter into consciousness? Two small but important pieces of evidence from the early sixteenth century acquire significance for what is said, who said it, and what they tell us about the background and future directions of the North. While they are limited in their scope to ideas and moral adaptations – not treating the more material needs of a society – still in their reliance on religious qualities, they provide added indications that the new North/South divisions of thought were largely coterminous with the Reformation.

Somewhat surprisingly the first example comes from Machiavelli. He excoriated the Italian character for its fraudulence and dishonesty. (The French and the Spanish share in these qualities, but are somehow spared chastisement because they live in a more unified nation-state.) The disunity of Italy only makes more viable the practices of deceit. He praises the Northern Germans for their *bontà* (goodness, or common honesty) and their *religione*. To be sure, whatever he praises in the Germans may be regarded as dispraise of his native Italians. This is not only present in his *Discorsi*, but also in his *Ritratto delle cose della Magna* (I. 697–702), where German industry, thrift, and lack of conspicuous consumption contrast with the Italian inclination towards luxury. Machiavelli's description of German thrift has the humorous directness of the man on the street when he declares that for the clothes on their backs the Germans do not spend more than two florins in ten years. The result is that their money stays home and they do not have to import expensive goods. The German *Wirtschaftswunder* of the years following the Second World War would have been understandable to the early sixteenth-century commentator. Machiavelli would affirm that they too are not concerned with the *bella figura*. Machiavelli is not speaking from ignorance, as Hegel himself sees revolution emerging from the "time-honored sincerity of the German people" (*Philosophy of History* 414).

They would both affirm the half-truth of the common saying (somewhat altered) that the farther one is from Rome, the closer one is to God. Giovanni Boccaccio, in the second story of the first day of his *Decameron*, inverts this perception in the story of Abraham the Jew who is accustomed to hearing of the sins of Rome. Giannotto, a friend, tries to persuade Abraham to convert to Christianity, but the latter is unwilling unless he can see for himself whether Rome lives up to its reputation. In the face of this insistence Giannotto fears his cause is lost. Abraham makes haste to Rome and finds it to be the swill of licentiousness and vice that he had expected, only more so. But this discovery has an unexpected effect. It can be called the "inverted miracle conversion." If the Catholic church can be growing throughout the world, despite this corruption, it must be the recipient of the Holy Spirit, Abraham concludes, and he converts.

While it is rightly customary to oppose Machiavelli and Erasmus (as Cassirer has so significantly shown), in some ways Erasmus joins his Italian compeer (whom he never mentions) in this particular assessment and, as it turns out, in several others as well. However, these apparent alignments are found in the work *Julius Exclusus*, whose single authorship by Erasmus is in dispute (see the full argument of this complex issue in the introduction by Michael J. Heath, *CWE* v.27. 157–63). Pope Julius II, whom Erasmus had seen resplendent in military glory enter the conquered Bologna at the head of his army, is defending his version of the papacy against the spiritual foundations of Christianity. He turns religious ethics on its head and unwittingly condemns himself and justifies his exclusion from heaven. He, too, entertains a North-South bias, but in his vocabulary the South is more modern because it tries to live according to the new ethical dispensations of the modern world, with whose new morality Julius's papacy complies, while the reformist North, by trying to restore the pristine ethics of an earlier Christianity, is antiquarian. W.K. Ferguson, looking from the other end of the telescope, stresses the long-range consequences in North-South relations because of this lapse in Church government. "The preoccupation of the papal Curia with temporal politics during these crisis years made it peculiarly unfitted to combat the spiritual revolution that broke out in Germany and that, within two generations, separated half of Northern Europe permanently from the Church of Rome."[1]

A history of early modern and modern times can be written by following the successive consolidation and replacements of nation-states. Portugal, leading the way in maritime expansion and exploration, was absorbed by Spain in 1580. But the first true challenges to a pre-eminent power were the uprisings of the Huguenots in France, resulting in eight wars followed by eight edicts, which certainly had an impact on the Dutch rebellion against Spain that followed beginning in 1572 (Israel 169–230).[2] This important trauma and resolution in France will be deferred, however, to chapter 9, where the edict of Nantes and tolerance will be given fuller attention.

In chapter 2, I indicated the obstacles that needed to be overcome before evangelical religious groups could move to direct action and rebellion, and why this outburst of insurgency originated within the development of Protestant groups. But a sense of the drama involved may be gained by showing three crucial characters in action. These protagonists are Philip II, the Duke of Alba, and William, Prince of Orange. Much is revealed about the issues of the changing times through the entanglements of these three personages. Their involvements explain why William, a genuine man of rectitude, the shining example of what was best in the system of vassalage, while not an intellectual, was still an extremely intelligent, skilful, and insightful man who was able to elude the many traps and lures set for him by the powers of Spain. He was what indeed he became, the father of his country, but not a country comprised of the unified seventeen provinces, but rather one divided by the seven provinces to the north of the three rivers, anchored by Holland and Zeeland, and by the provinces to the South, including Brabant and Flanders. He was never able to realize his grand scheme of unification, but that was mainly due to the actions of Spain and the reactions of the divided provinces, so different in their cultures and history. Thus it happened that it was in the Netherlands that the first important and lasting North/South divide occurred.

To understand the Duke of Alba one has merely to consult a record of his exploits; a summary caption of his character may be had from the portrait by Antonis Mor (who found a patron in Philip II), now hanging in the Royal Museum of Beaux-arts in Brussels. This painting brilliantly captures the methodical and savage cruelty of this very powerful military leader. He practiced a policy of intimidation by terror; he set examples by means of massacre. In the South, the city of Mechelen, which had opened its gates to Orange, met with serious reprisals upon the subsequent advent of Alba, who quite simply slaughtered many of its citizens. The other cities of the South absorbed this message and fell into line quickly. In the North he continued the same brutal policies. In Zutphen hundreds of its citizens perished under Alba's onslaught and in Naarden the entire population – men, women, and children – were put to the sword (with only a few escaping by nightfall). But in the North the reaction to these atrocities was different. Rather than inducing submission, Alba's cruelties only stiffened the backs of the largely Protestant (and Reformist) cities. The policy of intimidation through terror did not succeed and thus intensified the first North/ South divide. As an historical aside, one can also wonder why – with the histories of siege warfare well known – commentators can continue to insist that Guernica was the first case of warfare being conducted against a civilian population. That was the entire purpose of siege warfare: by starvation and bombardment to break a valued urban link of the opposition's strength.

With his Proclamation (August 1580) proscribing William of Orange, confiscating his properties, holding his son as a practical hostage in Spain, offering 25,000 crowns for his capture or death as well as a possible peerage, and the prior absolution of any and all crimes, Philip II had bared his fangs. In so doing he made several errors. He showed that the enemy was not rogue representatives of the King, but the King himself, thus justifying attack against him as he behaved in a most unworthy manner. He went against the advice of Alexander Farnese, the Prince of Parma, who succeeded the recalled Alba, and who warned that this Proclamation would only serve to make a martyr of Orange and add to his mystique. But most importantly, in William of Orange he got both the right man and the wrong man.

He got the right man because most certainly Orange was at the political and military centre of the Dutch revolt against Spanish rule. He was the catalyst and the glue, the man on the spot, urging threatened cities to hold out, canvassing for monies to pay soldiers and doing his utmost to encourage the besieged to hold on (the great example of Zutphen). To have eliminated William would have crippled the Dutch cause, upon whose shoulders rested the burden of the rebellions. The centrality of his position is indicated by the many traps meant to lure him into a place where he could be captured (lures that he was always sharp-witted enough to elude) and by the attempts to poison him. Finally the attempts succeeded when William fell to an assassin's bullet in July 1584. Assassination and outright slaughter seem to have been weapons of choice in the late sixteenth and early seventeenth centuries (not unlike America in the 1960s). A bullet is thought to be more effective than a ballot.

But Philip also picked the wrong man, a man stalwart in his sense of rectitude, supported by his firm conviction of the rights and privileges to which he made his oath of vassalage, and who, in the face of oppression, made others constantly aware of the common human rights of freedom of conscience and liberty. That is, the ancient sense of liberties was on its way to acquiring the larger sense of Liberty itself. His response was immediate and confidently managed. There are however flaws imputed to the *Apologie*, his response which appeared almost immediately in December 1580 after the King's Proclamation.[3] But on further scrutiny these can be disallowed. H. Wansink, the editor of the very handy edition of the rapidly produced English version of the *Apologie* (also containing instructive associated papers, including the king's Proclamation), finds William's "onslaught" on the King to be "vicious and groundless." But given the level of vituperation common to the time, it seems quite tame, and not unjustifiable in the context of the accusations and death warrant contained in the king's original. Another accusation against the *Apologie* is that it seems to have been written by committee. That there were other hands involved in its composition is beyond question; it was authored by court-chaplain Villers in the original French edition, with assistance by French Huguenots, including Hubert Languet and Plessis du Mornay. But any charge that it had all the defects of a committee's joint efforts seems groundless because this work (even in the cumbersome English version) has a cogency, force, and continuous drive not common to committee compositions. Moreover, while other hands were indeed involved it nevertheless bespeaks the character and firmness, the honesty and directness of William himself. Here we have a true register of his character.

While essentially given to solutions that appealed to the political mind, William was in his leanings clearly Protestant, even Lutheran. This might be seen in his strong advocacy of the right to marriage among the clergy. While being an early defender of some tolerance shown to Catholics, he later came to accept severe restrictions against them, a decision made on the basis of principle. Catholics and their clergy swear two oaths, one to the Pope and another to their country. Invariably at this time – and one could say, as William does, particularly after the bulls of Boniface VIII – the first took precedence. To him then, it is hardly reasonable "that any such people should enjoy a privilege, by means of which they would deliver the country into the enemies' hands." This brings us face to face with one of the widespread judgments of toleration's limitations. In modern terms this resolution means that no State has the right to commit suicide or to assist in its own hanging – by so doing it forfeits its right to be a State. The Huguenots could also support this proposition because they did not owe allegiance to a separate state (Geneva) but desired a modicum of the privileges of all Frenchmen. Seeing into the noxious doctrines of Boniface VIII, which Dante attacked so vehemently, William further argues against the multiplication of bishoprics throughout the Netherlands as this increase in number of dioceses is merely a ploy to extend the secular powers of the Inquisition. William, then, through his denunciation of the Spanish atrocities, his revelation of the duplicities and plots of Philip II, his early and clear-sighted opposition to the widening spread of the Inquisition under the guise of apparently religious purposes, was an early formulator of *la leyenda negra*.

To What Extent Climate?

In the descriptions by Machiavelli and Erasmus the North/South dichotomy is implied but not fully developed. Later in the sixteenth century, after the disturbances in Germany, the civil wars in France, and the wars of rebellion in the Netherlands – well after the death of the two great figures from an earlier epoch (Machiavelli d. 1527, Erasmus d. 1536) – there emerged a much fuller inclination to examine the North/South dichotomy both in scope and details. The efforts of Jean Bodin (1530–96) and Giovanni Botero (1540–1617) contributed greatly to the discussion. Their extremely popular books of statecraft, Bodin's *Les Six Livres de la République* (1576) as well as his earlier *Methodus ad facilem cognitionem historiarum* (I recommend the translation and introduction by Pierre Mesnard, *La méthode de l'histoire* 1941) and Botero's *Ragione di Stato* (1589) find the origin of causes, the reasons for behaviour in the variables of climatology. As cartographers they are tinkerers and gadgeteers, shuffling latitudes, juxtaposing human character traits, giving advice to lawmakers and rulers about natural dispositions, and explaining how awareness of such traits should enter into the deliberations of government. Climatologists nevertheless generate some interest because they draw attention to the abiding pressures of the North/South divide and they do so adhering to a particular method. But they are important not for what they say but for when they say it.

Although a jurist, Bodin is a humanist, repeating the oft-heard *rinascimentale* pledge to introduce new arguments beyond those that are commonly accepted (he cites some sixteen authorities, including Hippocrates and Aristotle). To be sure, experience tells us that the people of the North are taller and stronger, while those from the South are *plus faibles*. But he asks in the *Method*, where are the boundaries established? How far do they extend? These are questions waiting in the shadows which no one has brought to light (*La Méthode*, 69–72). He does draw dividing lines, and not a few, extending not only from North to South, but also from East to West, many with their own subdivisions.[4]

Bodin with some fussiness divides the globe into distinct areas north of the equator. The first zone of thirty degrees is the torrid, or southern, the next is the temperate zone, and the third of thirty degrees is the northern. It is the first and the third that usually (but not finally) square off in opposing contrasts. People of the North are larger and generate more internal heat. Consequently they have greater appetites in order to fuel their strength and war-like capabilities. They are more brutal in their punishments, but more phlegmatic by temperament. The people of the South do not win by force but rather by cleverness (they are more *rusé*). They gain by diplomacy what they have lost by war. When the southerners go north to battle they are invigorated by the refreshing cold but when the northerners head south they suffer from heat exhaustion (*Six Books* V.i 146–7). The northerners are chaste and modest while the southerners are libidinous. They need to be supplied by a harem, while the northerners are monogamous. None of these speculations is earth-shattering. Yet, what is striking is the utmost seriousness with which he culls his evidence from esteemed historical sources, only to come up with observations some of which are nothing more than old wives' tales, the kind of banal generalizations that are often uttered with a grim certitude. Despite his interest in bringing to light an exactitude that was not present before, his method is still to classify people by regions, which is nothing less than racialistic stereotyping, the kind of confident generalities that have troubled the closely contingent countries of Europe for centuries.

But as we have repeatedly observed, some binary divisions seek resolution by splitting the difference. Bodin's incursion into geography is no exception, as in most cases he locates the optimal conditions not in the extremes but rather in the intermediate temperate zone (where incidentally France might be found – *Six Books* 148). What northerners win by force and the people of the South by cleverness, the people of the temperate zone gain by a middling (*médiocrement*) mixture of both those qualities. This is why the people of the middle zone have established great empires and have flourished in arms and law and in all those institutions and virtues associated with public order (148). This point is repeated (as are others) practically verbatim in *La Méthode* (95). After having played his hand – "We have said that in general terms southern races are contrary to northern races" – his conclusions are qualified by his many uses of "in general," by the clarification that his meaning extends only to "inclinations" and not totality of character, and by the variety of elements brought in for consideration – "winds, humidity, the soil, the influence of laws and customs," not only climate. Thus, after having invoked the great dualisms of North and South, he introduces so many variables into the discussion that it is practically impossible to define any reliable system of preconditions.

Giovanni Botero, in his widely read *Reason of State*, resorts to the same politics of geography; for instance, people who live in the South are cunning but not bold, while Northerners are bold but not cunning. Like Bodin he finds the true treasure in the *juste milieu* (*Reason of State* 38–9). Unlike Bodin, Botero does not ransack the ancients for every possible opinion. This is a book that culls maxims fit for a prince's consideration. Yet his lists, like Bodin's, are given to overly subtle subdivisions such as including the East and West within the latitudinal compress, as well as the Southeast and the Northwest each with its own characteristics (which in geographically large countries such as the United States might have some cogency).Venturing closer than Bodin to the conditions of his contemporary world, Botero attributes to the South some "speculative and subtle" heresies, such as disputes over the divine or human nature of Christ, while to the North he credits attacks on more material things, like fasting, penitence, the celibacy of the priesthood; as Northerners are lovers of liberty, they "deny" the authority of the Papacy (39–40). As with Bodin, the North parties with Bacchus while the South clings to Venus. This work, while more interesting than a book on changes in the weather, might be better understood as another Advice to the Monarch, but one in which matters other than statecraft enter into judgment.

Botero himself exposes the many inadequacies – if not fallacies – of climatology. First, while maintaining that there are singular characteristics peculiar to North and South, the ideal characteristic is always somewhere in between. This provision collapses the dualism that he proposed to exploit. His intent to utilize the North and South polarity fails in the same way as did Bodin's recourse to the *tertium quid* and the arguments offered in *Dualisms* (4–5). They are like the disputes over mind and matter, subject and object, which are not ultimately disputes at all, because in reality they must merge and come together. They are obliging terms, their meanings being sufficiently elastic to permit various configurations to occur. Each represents the limitations of polar opposites and is rendered deficient by the middle term that assumes their better qualities. The end of such dualistic principles is found in the absorption of their oppositions into a third force. They only truly express themselves by means of fusion and not separation, while true dualisms express their key counter characteristics in separation.

Second, it is Botero's extensive use of geographic subdivisions that exposes another inadequacy of climatology. There should be changes of character for every substantial grouping of latitudes and longitudes. Such micromanagement would soon result in hordes of subtle character differences that explode the entire thesis. The multitude of geographic instances are too many not to fail. With such logic the real representatives of the North must be many more than the group that George Orwell humorously singles out.[5] Third, if climate is stable and unchanging (evidence shows that it is not) how is it that the fortunes of national characters undergo historical change? If climate is not stable, how can it be expected to produce the same characteristics? In short, climatic changes, like all organic metaphors, have little to do with the advancement or decline, or even the characteristics, of cultures.

Voltaire exposed this very same inadequacy in his *Dictionnaire*.[6] Why do we meet not cultural consistency but rather the vicissitudes of national pre-eminence, decline itself? Why does Athens not continue to produce its Aristotles, or Rome its Ciceros? – "… le climat n'a pas changé." He does concede some power to climate, but attributes to government one hundred times more, and to religion associated with government that much and more again (264–5).

Nevertheless, despite its gaping inconsistencies, the theory of climatic influence persisted down to the great Baron de Montesquieu who in the mid-eighteenth century devoted four chapters of his *L'Esprit des Lois* (1748) to climate. D'Alembert, in his somewhat lax description of Montesquieu's work, decides to settle for a bromide, claiming that while one cannot attribute all causality to climate, it would be wrong to strip it of any influence. The same argument was offered by Mme de Staël (see above). Adam Gopnik, writing in *The New Yorker* (29 October 2012) on "the renaissance of geographic history," can rightly wonder, "Are there any rules to this game?" Even Hegel finally settles for an opportune and unconvincing mix: the ideal climate is neither North nor South but "north temperate." Such incuriosity of thought, avoiding specifics (perhaps indicative of d'Alembert but certainly not Hegel) is strenuously upbraided by Voltaire in "Climat," where he insists that historical change depends upon changing circumstances – institutions of government and religion – and character, which is moulded by these historical causes. Ruling over all is the sense of time's vastness and the changes brought in its wake. This leads him to one of his most spectacular and daring visions: "peut-être," he writes, "les Américains viendront un jour enseigner les arts aux peuples d'Europe" (*Dictionnaire* 265).

Baron de Montesquieu (1685–1755) also emphasizes climatology, but as a latecomer to the argument he has to deal with the problem revealed through the works of Bodin and Botero. It tends to be one of repetition. How often do we have to read that in the North we find people who are stern, vigorously active, modest and chaste, while the Southerners are, because of the warm weather, lazy, clever or tricky, and lascivious. Later Anglo-Dutch-American adherents to racialistic theories will find here their intellectual ancestors. Some one hundred years later, commentators not without their own biases, and writing with less nuance, will still depend upon the backdrop of North-South climatologies.[7]

In order to avoid constant repetition, the climatologists, especially Botero, have recourse to subdivisions along the latitudinal lines, which are a disadvantage rather than an advantage. Montesquieu's contribution is not so much in his conclusions (which we have heard before), but in his methodology, the means by which he arrives at his affirmations. His work shows the Baconian accumulation of evidence and the growth of experimental science in the more than 150 years that separate his procedures from those of Bodin and Botero.

In his wide search for examples Montesquieu practically covers the globe; his *L'Esprit des lois* (1748) is an example of universal history (to Voltaire's regret and irritation). He does succumb to climatology, but his approach (like those of Bodin and Botero) is far from monolithic. He prescribes different kinds of laws for different climates. Basic divisions remain between North and South and cold and hot weather conditions. Yet all the differences come back to human physiology and the laws of contraction and expansion (474–80). The cold of the northern zones compresses the *"fibres,"* thus the blood courses through these narrower channels with greater force, returning to the heart with greater power. This added power of the heart has its effect on the northern personality. Greater energy means greater self-confidence, which also means "plus de franchise, et moins de soupçon, politique et ruse," qualities of frankness and openness which have been associated with the increased "dynamism" of the North. Warm weather has the opposite effect. It expands the *"fibres"* thus returning the blood to the heart more languidly, making for a weakness of heart, or courage, a lack of hardiness in enterprise. This type of person fears everything because he fears that he is capable of nothing. Unlike Botero, Montesquieu draws no confessional conclusions from these descriptions but they are there to be drawn.

These speculations are supported by ventures into experimentation. He studies the tongue of a sheep. When it is frozen its papillae contract within their hairy sheaths. This means it requires extraordinary stimulation in order to generate a reaction. It thus follows that people of the northern, colder clime are slower in movement, heavy, in need[8] of extra stimulation in order to react. They have no quick wit. Once these same papillae are opened under warm conditions they are responsive to multiple, even slight stimulation. They thrive in a feast of the senses and like expansive Southerners (according to Hippocrates, Bodin, Botero and Montesquieu) find love on every breeze, where the contracted souls of the North have trouble detecting the signals. Yet all the differences come back to human physiology and the laws of contraction and expansion.

In his *Idées Républicaines* (517–24) Voltaire subjects both Rousseau's *Contrat social* and Montesquieu's *L'Esprit des Lois* to rigorous analysis. The first he treats as an enemy (indeed an opponent in a dualism), negating his argument when not resorting to scorn and ridicule. His dispute with Montesquieu is conducted on much friendlier terms, finding the aristocrat's major fault to be an expression of strength; he has too many examples, thus obscuring any central argument. "Je suis fâché que ce livre soit un labyrinthe sans fil" (*Dictionnaire* 897). There is no guy-wire, no conductor leading to any thesis. His search for a variety of test cases reduces the clarity of his plan (Art. XLIX). *"Mais à quoi bon étaler toutes ces digressions?"* Voltaire asks, what's the purpose of displaying all these digressions? But there is an even greater dispute, greater because it shows Voltaire's true purpose as an historian, as a searcher of exemplary lessons from the past as ways of meeting questions of the present. Here his deep sense of the variety of historical examples joins with his innate scepticism concerning "general principles." Hardly has Montesquieu enunciated one such general rule, than history opens before him and shows him one hundred contrary examples (*Dictionnaire* 898). The verb is enticing, suggesting the readiness of history to show its quite lavish and abundant spread. Still, *malgré tout*, Voltaire welcomes him because of attacks he has endured from the *fanatiques* at those very places in his writing where he deserves the gratitude of humankind. He wages war against superstition, and inspires *la morale* (907).

Chapter Seven

Centring the Great Bases in Thought

Hegel's thought, detailed and comprehensive, is central to the expansive growth of Christian liberty. Born in 1770, he was ideally placed to summarize what had gone before and by the power of his thought and his psychological acuity to open the way for much of what was to come, especially in the work of Weber and Cassirer. Harald Höffding remarks on Hegel's "realistic nature," which despite his speculative and abstract method "wanted to re-think the fullness of life, to translate it into the form of thought" (*A History of Modern Philosophy*, v.2 175). This erudite Danish historian of philosophy is obliged to register this anomaly in Hegel's works since it becomes a point of contention. He follows this stirring attestation of Hegel's sense of "reality" with a statement of regret over Hegel's apparent reliance on the dialectical method, of thesis-antithesis and synthesis. "The very method which he [Hegel] believed would lead him to the goal [of reconciling the subjective world of the inner spirit with the objective structures of society] prevented his thoughts from attaining the form and foundation such as could ensure them the lasting significance which they deserve" (Höffding, v.2 175). Anyone coming fresh to a reading of Hegel's *Philosophy of History* (trans. J. Sibtree, 1956, source of all quotations in this volume) might find the critical application of dialectic to be strange, given the infrequency of its occurrence. According to John N. Findlay, in *Hegel: A Re-examination of His Thought* (a properly modulated, finely tuned summary of Hegel's thought), dialectical terms "are in fact not frequently used by Hegel." In Findlay's introduction to Frederick Weiss's *Hegel, The Essential Writings* (1974), he goes even further. The famous triad (he translates it as Being, Nothing, and Becoming), which, so far from being typical of Hegel's system, is "only the abstract nonsense whose clearing away allows the system to begin." Like Höffding, Findlay would credit Hegel's permanent hold on our imagination to the remarkably brilliant insights that his theory yields and not to the fully detailed application of the theory itself (Findlay, *A Re-examination* 79, 82).

Christian liberty is Hegel's great motivating principle in the advancement of freedom itself. It has proved to be the missing link in the evolution towards complete freedom of conscience, and receives in Hegel's thought its full justification and support. It is an argument derived from the Gospels, used to discredit the practices of the Church. Its origins are in the German world which introduced into the Roman world over which it presided an entirely new concept, that of "the absolute self-determination of subjectivity." It is from this seed that later Christian freedom would grow (in Sibtree 343). This occurred during the reign of Charles V, indeed in Charles's very presence at Luther's greatest moment at Worms. The secular world here begins to gain some recognition of its own intrinsic worth when the missing link is provided. "The consciousness of independent validity is aroused through the restoration of Christian liberty" (344). There is no mistaking Hegel's meaning here, but this concept means more than it appears to convey. Christian liberty is a concept on the way to another form of thought and that is Thought's independent validity.

Henceforward no specimen of customary morality or traditional usage remains unless it passes the test of rational inspection with the aid of the Holy Spirit. But the necessary missing step to fuller understanding of this process was Christian liberty. "Not till this era is the freedom of spirit realized (i.e., the Reformation)" (345).

There is a logical and necessary connection between the restoration of Christian liberty and the attainment of freedom of spirit (345). A necessary correlative condition was the decline of the Church into "mediated materiality." It forsakes its role as guide to the spirit but continues to insert itself between humankind and God. People are led as if they were children (hence Luther's appeal to the adult consciousness). "A condition the very reverse of freedom is intruded into the principle of freedom itself" (379).

In his thought Hegel combines the true dimensions of character and causality and understands from the inside the psychological and historical bases of the North/South divide. He addresses large spans of time and the driving ideas within those times. Hegel confronts the basic question of this study: Why, he asks, did the Reformation, so essential to the development of the modern world, not find a home in the

Romance countries of the South? Hegel's visionary history relies on his analysis of the "character" of the South, which existed in contradiction with itself, a kind of *disharmony* (*Entzweiung* – and the phrase is italicized, 421). The Southern character exhibits the absence of totality of spirit, having no introversion of the meditative soul upon itself; it is alienated from itself. Hence there can be no union of the secular and the religious, but instead there is a kind of resignation, or even a taste for cynical witticisms. Their inner life is not their own; instead they have obediently consigned it to the guidance of the Church. Unlike the Protestants of the North they have lost their independent wholeness of being. They are not at one with themselves or the world. Hegel shows, not only in his large, systematic program but also in the particulars that move the souls of people, masterful insight, superior to that of Bodin, Botero, and Montesquieu.

Hegel observes that the Reformation entailed political as well as ecclesiastical change, anticipating and countering Spenle's contention far in advance (see below p. 89). Like Milton, Hegel thought the political and the ecclesiastical inseparable from but also implicated in processes of growth, allowing for a certain flexibility of judgment according to the circumstances. From the very start some elements of the Protestant reform rebelled not only against spiritual but against secular authorities. Anabaptists expelled the bishop in Munster and had a hand in unleashing the peasants' rebellion, much to Luther's displeasure. And, sensing the rightness of Luther's reaction, Hegel nevertheless deduces that the world was not yet ready for a transformation of its political conditions consequent to its ecclesiastical reformation (419); hence the coexistence of the reformed religions with a "limited monarchy."

Such historical pauses recur in Hegel's thought. His domain is history, philosophically understood. This principle applies to the interpretation of the actions of his beloved Luther, who "has secured to mankind spiritual freedom and the Reconciliation [of the Objective and the Subjective] in the concrete; he triumphantly established the position that man's eternal destiny [his spiritual and moral position] must be wrought *in himself* [cannot be … a work performed *for him*]." When it comes to matters of salvation people must carry their own water. All the prayers of others, the programs of the Church, the doctrine of "works" are of no avail if one does not understand in his inner being the meaning of the way (415). But the grounds for this belief rested on a deeply scrutinized and critically studied text, the Bible. The basis of Luther's faith is not *sola scriptura* but Scriptures read by a mind attuned by the Holy Spirit and aided by reason (417); for instance, Luther preferred the Epistles over the Gospels, and had only a distaste for Revelations, saying if something is to be revealed it ought to be clear. What was needed for a full realization of freedom was an opening up of the grounds of investigation to the premise of Thought, the inward acceptance or rejection to which every dogma and practice must be referred (441–2). Reformed thought requires this further substantial reformation if it is to become what Voltaire called *la morale universelle*. It must move from its lengthy phase of opposition to the objective world, to a reconciliation, that is, to the full participation of interiority with the public world, the goal and the function of the Enlightenment.

But it works the other way as well, fortifying the argument that was referred to above as "negative proofing." The maligned Southern countries failed twice: in religious and political rebellion. And the two failures are connected. Their political dimensions remained bound to the fetters of "religious slavery," lacking interiority, which assessment Hegel caps with a powerful edict: "there can be [no] Revolution without a Reformation" (453). As one ponders the failed revolutions (as well as failed countries) since Hegel's time, and the successful ones, that uncompromising formula acquires strong evidentiary support.

Hegel's profound thought combines the public and the private, maintaining that on the one hand, through the struggles of history, people can redeem the secular, rendering it capable of carrying the body of truth (422), making it possible for humankind to be at one with themselves. Morality and justice in the state are also divinely sanctioned and justified by the endowments of the human spirit, the two at last forming a unity. The elevation of marriage (including that of the clergy) and the family lead to active involvement in the community, the prime engine for the growth of industry and trade. All these resacralized elements of modern society complete the historical purpose of the reconciliation of God and the World. The modern world as we know and honour it, is here revealed and attained, and is quite different from Weber's "disenchantment." At first it required abstraction, but finally abstractions are realized in ordinary life. Thought in itself, by itself, replaces the early humanistic eager reliance on the Book and authoritative citation. The project of Luther is fully developed in Hegel's vision. Luther's true heir is not Nietzsche but Hegel. Christian liberty thus opens the way to what is chiefly valued in modern society, and that is active, intellectual justice.

John N. Findlay shows the roots of a more complex modern thought in Hegel, one philosophical and another historical. Philosophy has become thought about thought, but thought that is always escaping, slipping away from itself. It involves the negation of the first surmise. This is actually a three-step process, involving the negation of the negation. In order to avoid the trap of infinite regress it returns to capture the elusive reality of things, from which thought is constantly escaping. Thus Hegel is an acolyte of history, but history profoundly understood and not the history of common understanding. He sees fundamental principle as active in history, but people function oblivious to the ulterior purpose they are fulfilling. In contrast, Luther had ample opportunity to reflect on the doors he pushed open beyond his conscious intent. T.S. Eliot also shows Hegelian influence (among others). The Heraclitian fragment heading *Four Quartets* announces that the Logos is perceivable but that the *polloi* live as if they had a law of their own (or unto themselves). Behaviour is purposeful but ignorant of its own ends, which are revealed only when fulfilled, "if at all." "Either you had no purpose / Or the purpose is beyond the end you figured / And is altered in fulfillment" (*Little Gidding* I). Hegel shows little of the humility of Eliot's thought. Rather, he issues trumpet blasts, "Man is destined to be free."

But it is exactly this powerful clarity of purpose that explains the current fascination with Hegel's *The Philosophy of History*, where one finds the best of Hegel's philosophical insights into the history of the world – ancient and modern – without the imposition of unduly complex and intricate procedural gradations. This clarity of reception is also partly due to the fact that what became a book had actually been a series of public lectures. In *The Philosophy of History* there are some minor references to the three stages of development and the necessity of negation. But this is because that work is already the product of the variety in the stages of Hegel's thought. Africa is passed over as the never-to-be and America is the not-yet, but they have little bearing upon the development of freedom. Asia yields to Greece but that is a simple passage, with a great difference, not due to direct negation. Obviously as one moves diachronically through cultures a succeeding period will present contested differences in comparison with the preceding, with no sense that the present negates the preceding or even that it grows out of it. It can be of an entirely different vintage, representing two diverse cultures. Virgil, for instance, can give due recognition to the values of Greece while at the same time asserting the values of Roman culture. In the development of freedom, from the Reformation of the German world to the Enlightenment and up through Hegel's contemporary moment, there is continuity. In *Dualisms* yet another relationship is discernible, that of a lateral poetics, a cross-rivalry, where opposites are never reconciled but rather held fast, down through the ages, not even joined by death, because they represent values perpetually at odds, and thus do not lend themselves to any dialectic.

Under close scrutiny one can discern the image in Hegel's mind (which is suggested by Findlay in his foreword to Frederick Weiss's study), an overcoming of the divorce between the attachments of mind and the occupation of the senses, of the disharmony he perceives in the Southern and Catholic mentality. Thus even his invocation of a *Zeitgeist* may, within narrow restrictions, have its justification. To fall short of the demands of the times is not, as Höffding suggests above, a simple anachronism. Truth may not be chronological, but it clearly involves the acceptance of certain challenging and new principles, such as the four concepts. The ideal becomes embodied in the daily and the mundane. There is no divorce between thought and action. The grounding of the universal in the subjective and immediate is the remedy for more than what had been ailing Spain; Hegel is thereby prescribing medicine for a European illness.

A quite dramatic yet logical follower of Hegel is Max Weber. Despite all their differences of methodology, Weber remains within the orbit of German thought and accepts the essential point of the religious origins of some of the principles of the modern world. His admittedly contested thesis of the connection between the "protestant ethic" and the "spirit of capitalism" can avoid the charges of error (which seem more like petty nuisances) but is guilty of another charge – that of limited perspective.

While defending Weber's overall thesis it is possible to expand his argument and extend its scope. His classic work, *The Protestant Ethic and the Spirit of Capitalism,* was first published in two parts in a German journal in 1904–5, and revised for publication in his *Collected Works,* 1920–1. Since then his arguments have been picked at, but not picked apart. Among the more recent critiques is that advanced by Felipe Fernández-Armesto and Derek Wilson in *Reformations* (1996, 276–89). Most of their arguments have been rebutted by David S. Landes in his *The Wealth and Poverty of Nations* (1998), where he openly differs with Weber's "detractors" who find his arguments "implausible and unacceptable." Landes takes issue on the "empirical" level, citing as examples France, Switzerland, Germany, and England where Protestant merchants and manufacturers played leading roles in "trade, banking and industry."

He also challenges arguments on the "theoretical" level questioning the assertion that Protestants succeeded in producing a "new kind of man – rational, ordered, diligent, productive" (177). Going beyond Weber, Landes attributes this ascendancy to two factors: an emphasis on literacy among the Protestant families and the new sense of time (178). Weber's critics miss the forest for the trees, while some of his defenders (Landes among them) do not delve too deeply into the actual mechanisms of change that Weber employs to justify his larger conclusions. His attackers assail him by referring to the exceptions (that might prove the rule), while his defenders admire the large scale Weber, the Weber who must be read *grosso modo*, who cites astonishing cultural contrasts and historical developments. They are both correct and incorrect, although the defenders have more ground to stand on.

The Protestant Ethic and the Spirit of Capitalism is a high wire act of many challenging flips, an enchanting book that describes a world of disenchantment. Weber's thesis stands out because its scope is so prodigious, addressing a major change in historical values. Fundamentally, his classic statement is devoted to the active role of religious thought in social life, a focus which allies him with his American compeer, William James.[1] In the Middle Ages acquisition was considered to be a product of covetousness. We remember the third beast, the *lupa* (she-wolf) that sent Dante hopelessly reeling back down the hill of contemplation. The urge for acquisition was then considered sheer turpitude, or at best, barely tolerable. But by the standards of Benjamin Franklin, the prototype of this new man, acquisition is considered a moral virtue, the sign of diligence. This new man is a figure who has attained social credibility; he is not a buccaneer, nor an adventurer, not even a "traditionalist." Rather, his program of acquisition is calm, calculated, and well-organized, and as a result he is to be honoured and respected. The wastrel or spendthrift was not only disgraced and discredited (already regarded in literary terms as the foppish dandy – the heir of the useless aristocrat) but in his fallen condition, was seen as a person well on the way to Hell, or worse, the living example of disastrous social scandal. In Benjamin Franklin's evaluations and advisories one sees the circle squared: one can win both success in this world and salvation in the next. Obviously the wastrel achieves neither. Far from inhabiting a tension-filled oppositional relationship, acquisition and Christian piety exist on the same scale of values. This was more than one individual's program; it was part of a new ethos, a larger Protestant ethic. While not accounting for every appearance of capitalism it does intensify the development of a particular brand of capitalism that came to thrive in the North. The virtuous plan of living contained the new business ethic, and the new business ethic promoted the virtuous life.

How did this change occur? Did it happen overnight, or was there some critical early stage of transfer whereby some religious sanction was given to worldly success? Here, *Les Promesses du monde* (1996) by Pierre Bouretz offers helpful explications of Weber's thought – thought that even admirers must acknowledge as enigmatic and paradoxical. For Weber this was the only way it could have happened. A kind of religious asceticism that had been appropriate for monastic communities, became an essential part of living and working in the secular world. This required nothing short of a revolution in the way people understood the attainment of salvation, involving methodical action in regard to earthly matters and the search for assurance as to the connection of the two (219). This transfer of qualities produced prosperity and approval, bringing diligence, honesty, and hard work to the trades and commerce that had formerly been thought to be less than honourable. A certain laxness was decried. Bouretz concludes that thus understood, the Calvinist version of Puritanism "représente sans aucun doute l'expression la plus achevée d'une religiosité désenchantée" (225), that is, a modern world without the need of magic formulae or sacraments, but which stood face to face with a rational world "denuded of all spirituality." A new business ethic emerged that represented the height of virtue, higher even than knighthood. And to those peoples and countries who despised the grind of daily industry, who fostered the *hidalgo* habits of mind and action, they were soon left in the rearguard, adrift in a society whose regimen no longer had a place for them. The sober knight of capitalist accumulation had replaced the soldier-adventurer as the hero of a new society. Money was the desideratum of social being, the currency of power. This code was not only appropriate for the financier (the real captain-treasurer of capitalism) but also throughout the world of business from artisan to tradesman to all those adopting the proprieties of bourgeois life. More than a change in handling, this was a change in typology, as new values were invested in a new figurehead. Such an enormous change of the social ordering was the reason that Rousseau in *Emile* urged that children of the gentry be taught a trade so as to be prepared for the coming upheaval.

Weber's thesis is both paradoxical and ingenious. The new business ethic thrived in precisely those countries where Calvinist Reformism had prevailed, particularly under the threatening logic of predestination. Bouretz calls this without any doubt the "decisive moment" (222). It was Weber's insight that the new capitalist ethic derived from responses required by this focus on predestination and with the harrowing sequential problem of determining whether one was among the elect. In a somewhat dubious distinction from Lutheranism, Bouretz writes that it is in the framework of daily existence, with its successes or failures, that the Calvinist is able to identify the signs of election, to disburden himself of the "anguish" of a disenchanted world, where there is no way to pierce the designs of heaven (223). The ordinary man requires the "mécanismes de réassurance psychologique" which can only be acquired by "works." But these are not the "works" that Luther discounted but rather in the Calvinist world "un véritable système d'action, méthodique, rationel et orienté par l'idée que c'est le succès dans ces oeuvres qui pourra être vécu comme signe d'éléction" (A veritable system of action, methodical, rational, directed by the idea that it is success in these works that can be regarded as a sign of election, 231). Put in more ordinary terms, the dilemma seems to have been resolved by simply storming the citadel; a strong conviction that one was among the elect was sufficient to indicate that one was so. One can think back to the self-assurance of Sartre's grandfather, who has so conducted his life and its affairs that he can harbor no self-reproach. Self-confidence – "pilgrim's pride" – removed all doubt and promoted a commitment to public endeavour. A process of rationalization is introduced which directs the religious towards the economic, and further still, towards the social, and then the political (227).

Weber's thesis can answer the question, "How does a type of activity that was in another time indifferent to salvation or even contrary to its ends, become a symptom of election?" (226). Nevertheless, it does require some agility to derive the Protestant ethic from the doctrine of predestination. Weber's assertion is most unlike Hegel's thesis, where the doctrine of human social freedom derived from the idea of Christian liberty. This is not to dismiss Weber's major argument. *North/South* shows some parallels, in fact, with Weber's argument; this is a story of development, of transformation, and of finding a pathway from one period to another. Like Weber's study it has its origins in the Reformation, but unlike Weber's it looks to the fuller qualities that emerged throughout the Reformation, which ultimately revealed their attraction and power in the Enlightenment. The approach of *North/South* is broader, highlighting the four qualities that receive special attention here, qualities that in Voltaire's opinion brought forth opulence as a by-product.

I make use of Weber's volume as a sort of counter-face, accurate in its outlines but debatable in its specifics. The masterful pages where Weber compares Calvin and Luther open up a second front, one in which *North/South* differs yet again in the details. In contrast to Luther (and Lutheranism), Calvinist reformers seemed to rise above, or place behind them, the passionate upheavals of spiritual struggle. Moreover, rather than suffering in solitude, one found solace in the efforts of a group, a collectivity. Was Tocqueville correct in assuming that Americans value equality over liberty? To this day, the willingness, or the emotional need, to be a "joiner," to find edification in groups that bring aid to the afflicted, the handicapped, and impoverished (thus not eluding a self-satisfaction that is only another indication of being among the elect), has been a defining part of the American character, for whom civic involvement has greater appeal than do the ambiguities of consciousness. Weber sees in Calvinism the virtues of self-control – a self-control that was diligent and vigilant. This he deems to be quite different from the more accepting attitude of Luther and Lutherans who were aware of and dependent upon the mysteries of the coming of grace. Oddly enough, then, out of self-preserving responses to predestination, the new (Weberian) Protestant ethic of self-confidence and self-control emerged. This armory of religious virtues – most prominent in Calvinism – spread to life in community and became the ethic so useful in the practice of capitalism. Calvin did not discover such qualities but under his guidance they took on as a whole the shape of an ethic, a regulatory system that found itself amenable to business success.

This diptych of Calvin and Luther is useful as it shows that there are other ways to achieve a similar end, that is, the transformation of a specifically religious conception of the world into a related but secularized version, a kind of intellectual or practical metamorphosis. In his insistence on the forward-moving qualities of Calvinist reformism, Weber has a tendency to make Luther more "traditional" and "medieval" than he actually was. To be sure, in regard to the central issue of a calling everyone must be dutiful and accepting of their station and lot in life. This is God's will. But this religious principle is given a polemical twist and Luther's anthropology assumes a more modern stance. Christian status does not depend upon station in life. Remarkably enough, where Calvinism has stratified election Luther has democratized salvation. The plowman may be as good a Christian as the priest, and the housewife as worthy in her faith as the bishop. There is no royalty in the kingdom of God; every soul must struggle with the issues of faith. The secure self-confidence of the Calvinist elect is not available to the spiritual struggle facing the true follower of Luther. The Lutheran soul does not share the self-control required, according to Weber, of the newly born Calvinist. Luther professes a divestment of ownership that is far different from the Calvinist appropriation. Consequently, in the northern provinces of the Netherlands, Calvinist supremacy brought a radicalization of its politics (quite useful in opposing Spain), but also a less tolerant attitude towards Jews, Catholics – and Lutherans. In the seventeenth century they completed the circle against which Rousseau remonstrated: installing a protestant papacy, forgetting their own roots in the Reformation, and causing profound and direful consequences for such powerful thinkers as Descartes and Spinoza, who were obliged either to suppress their works or to have them printed anonymously and in falsified places.

Weber's picture of Luther, while accurate in part, is one-sided, more like a profile than a true portrait. In fact, what he misses in Luther are precisely those qualities brought out in *Dualisms* (56–75). Luther shakes up the sacerdotal structures of the Church. He further evinces a bold assertiveness (as well as a compassionate awareness of the frailties of the flesh) when he advises the poor village pastor to marry the woman with whom he has been living. A newly acquired firmness sounds in Luther's voice, and it is this voice, this firmness, that will resonate throughout history. He urges the chagrined couples to stand by their consciences and their personal vows. They are free to abandon the social proprieties that Bouretz would see as a product of Weber's Calvinist perspective. He promises those who would follow his word that he will not lead them astray. "I have not the power of a pope, but I have the power of a Christian to help and advise my neighbor to escape from his sins and temptations." What Luther is advocating is a new freedom for the serious adult consciousness. "Therefore I declare that neither pope, nor bishop, nor any one else, has the right to impose as much as a single syllable of obligation upon a Christian man without his own consent." The phrase "nor any one else" (*necque ullam hominem*) following in the line from pope and bishop may refer to a clerical relation. Nevertheless the statement resonates powerfully, and its meaning will be extended beyond the purely ecclesiastical to civil matters as well. From Calvin we get the constraining armor of the buttoned-up capitalist; from Luther we get the powerful assent to freedom (hence, his favoured position with Hegel) without which even the "spirit of capitalism" cannot survive. Weber adheres to Calvin as the chief promulgator of the "modern" (!) ethic, but the same case at the personal level of the adult consciousness can and will be made for Luther. This contrast reveals the remarkable differences between the two phalanxes of the Protestant revolution. While it can be said that they advanced together, still in their afterlives profound differences showed themselves. The Calvinist upheld the social proprieties, while those more closely following Luther responded to the message of the individual conscience.[2]

The long journey of freedom took its first big steps in the time of the Reformation. As Hegel phrased it, under the Oriental despots, one was free; with the Graeco-Roman governments, some were free; with the Reformation, or at least according to its principles, all were free. The proposition of Christian liberty exerts a similar kind of liberation. Christian liberty is an active, living, effective concept that both liberates and empowers the soul, that is of great argumentative value in separating Church and State, religion and the magistrate, and that is generative in the development of civil liberties. This section could be subtitled "the Reformation and its transformations." The Renaissance (or Reformation) did not "wane," rather it was transformed. It raised the concepts that, when pursued and developed, spread their wings to larger freedoms. Nor was it a period of "transition." Between it and the Enlightenment, there existed a continuum. The refreshing idea of Christian liberty is at the core of this development. Despite interpretations of Hegel that affirm the contrary, there is no sense of negativity or rupture in Hegel's conception of Christian liberty. While there might be other concepts that explain this transformation, why not, invoking Ockham's razor, rely on the one that is user-friendly, readily present, opportune, and easy to follow and understand? It is also expansive, like a Lovejovian unit-idea joining hands with other forces and personages and thus undergoing its own transformation. Such is Christian liberty. In Milton's hands one can see the concept transformed, not only in itself but in the issues against which it is used as an argument. It both proclaims and prevents. This was the key concept that the Catholic world in the main eschewed.

Despite this substantial obstacle, the doctrine of Christian liberty would only increase in power and appeal, in fact becoming the more widespread doctrine of civil liberty. Yet it is this very continuous development that is challenged by Jean-Édouard Spenlé in his comment "bien à tort on a cru reconnaître dans la doctrine de Luther une formule anticipée de la liberté de conscience" (Truly it is an error ["bien a tort on a cru"] to attribute to Luther's doctrine an anticipation of liberty of conscience). But we can insist that the evidence already provided in its support is overwhelming.

Here we leap forward from the beginning to the fuller exploitation of the argument, with a brief glance at Voltaire and Rousseau, about whom much more may be said. In the hands of Voltaire and Rousseau the meaning of liberty has been applied to civic functions but its earlier birth in religious controversy is still clear. Voltaire announces that he is bringing to completion the work left *imparfait* by his *pères* of the Reformation (*Dualisms* 103). His intellectual purpose shows continuity. In *Lettres écrites de la montagne*, Rousseau gives lessons in the meaning of the Reformation to the elders of Geneva. "Where else does the genius of Protestantism lie, he argues, but in the issue that separated it from the Roman persuasion, and that was the forthright defense of personal freedom?" The elders are thus going against the very principles of the Reformation – Christian liberty – when they condemn him without a hearing. The psychological connection between the artistic and political freedoms of the Protestant countries and the stagnation (in many areas) of the South has to do with this fundamental principle. One cannot write with an overbearing force hovering over one's shoulder. Writer's block in such a context is not in front of one, on the blank paper, but behind one in the domineering presence. This is true psychologically and has been prevalent enough to make it obvious, whether in the context of external forces such as the Index, the Inquisition, Big Brother, or an ambience of political correctness. Such forces are diversionary, preventing the free flow into consciousness of the expressive energies that inhabit one. Rousseau converts this into a general principle, the origins of which clearly form the bases of Protestantism. In the Profession of Faith of the Savoyard Vicar, inserted in *Émile*, the vicar, in defending his return to the religion of his youth, emphasizes humankind's first duty: "nul n'est exempt du premier devoir de l'homme, nul n'a droit de se fier au jugement d'autrui" (625). "No one has the right to place his/her trust in the judgment of another." An individual's rooted responsibility derives from the principle of Christian liberty. So fundamental is this statement that Cassirer can only conclude, "There is no doubt that with these propositions Rousseau once more returned to the actual central principle of Protestantism" (*The Question of Jean-Jacques* 117). That is, inherently, Protestant Christian liberty is the eventual midwife of civil liberty. Consequently – and the new application to civil liberties is crucial – how can the elders of Geneva remain true to their calling and condemn Rousseau's works without a hearing? In most of America's patriotic anthems one finds the same transposition. The "Battle Hymn of the Republic" brings together the religious message of Christ with the struggle for human freedom: "As he died to make men holy, let us die that [all] be free." In *Patriotic Gore* Edmund Wilson argues that under the fiercely militant Calvinist ethos of the poem, Christ is peripheral and not stomping on any grapes of wrath (96). But he overlooks the theological prominence of Christ as the sacrificial son, and thus a model for those who are called to sacrifice themselves for the sake of freedom for others. "America the Beautiful" begins its second stanza by praising the "stern impassioned stress" of the pilgrims' feet "who beat a thoroughfare for freedom" across the wilderness. These are major and minor examples of the close connection between original Protestant doctrine as extolled by Luther, Christian freedom, and its inevitable development into a larger civic and political defence of freedom. The very first amendment to the American Constitution combines freedom of religion with freedom of speech. The next chapter will culminate with the influence of Milton and Mill on the expansion of the liberties protected in the First Amendment.

Chapter Eight

English Thought: John Milton, John Locke, and John Stuart Mill

There are other figures occupying critical positions in the passage from Erasmus to Voltaire and beyond. Some are warrior princes, William I, Prince of Orange, Oliver Cromwell, and Gustavus Adolphus; some are intellectual crown princes, Descartes, Bayle, and Spinoza. One such figure, who represents a major intervention, was John Milton. Yet another figure, who might seem to be out of phase here, is John Locke, in particular because of his *Letter Concerning Toleration*. In choosing to insert these two figures in the section on the various treatments of Christian liberty, I emphasize the radical change that had overtaken English Christian thought in the thirty-year period from Milton's *A Treatise of Civil Power in Ecclesiastical Causes* (1659) to Locke's letter on toleration (1689). Milton's intervention makes all the clearer the role that Christian thought has played in the development of the Enlightenment. It explains why some have criticized Locke for the absence of the liberal issues of a later period while others have been disappointed by his adherence to forms of Christianity that are not traditional. But the great middle road involves both, combining religious belief with liberal ethics. Christian liberty represented the great mutation from the one to the other; it shows the one gradually yielding place to the other. It is indeed the missing link that Weber, with his emphasis on predestination, does not provide.

Milton was far from being a way-station on the road from Erasmus to Voltaire. Like a giant he stands astride the middle third (and beyond) of English religious and political thought in the seventeenth century. He understood profoundly the concept of Christian liberty and fervently pursued its application to questions of civil liberty. He not only described it, he embodied it, and provided evidence of the mutually beneficial association of the literary imagination with some form of politicized energy. Milton was England's second greatest poet and a brilliant polemicist. He witnessed the sad depression within the ranks of Italian humanists. There is a conductive charge from the outside world of freedoms to the homely world of personal activity. Here, by force of his vivid imagination and keen understanding, his personal identification, and his powerful prose, Milton enters the historical argument to reveal the fuller developments of the original concepts. He knows of what he speaks and is able to follow in his life the dictates of his mind. In two works, *Areopagitica* (1648) and *A Treatise on Civil Power in Ecclesiastical Causes* (called analogous by Barbara Lewalski in an exemplary introduction), he wholeheartedly endorses Christian liberty as defining and defending the very principles of the Reformation itself. In each work Milton writes as a native son of Protestantism and of England as its original seed-bed (he has in mind Wyclif and the Moravian Hus, who had many followers in England). Such antecedents do not demean his role, rather they enhance it, revealing each as part of an ongoing stream; together they are as one. His birthright derives from England's identity as a premier Protestant nation. In *Areopagitica* he makes this allegiance specific, and in *Civil Powers*, it shows in the simplicity of the prose. *Areopagitica* is thickly brocaded linguistically, while ten years later the *Civil Power* is written in "plain English." There he is intent on stripping such terms as "blasphemy" and "heresy" of their foreign colouring in order to show what they mean in simple prose, where they become less intimidating (453–4). In each work, he establishes three fronts: Christian liberty, religious liberty, and civil liberties. In the second work the concept of Christian liberty is even more extensively refined and elaborated. *Civil Powers* embodies what the earlier advocated. Each work is devoted to showing both Christian liberty and religious liberty as being beyond censure or force from the civil authorities, as interference in these areas by a magistrate implies an Inquisition. It is because Milton gives voice to both kinds of liberty in his *Areopagitica* that the work has become a classic, a central document in the bringing together of Christian liberty with civil liberty, while at the same time immunizing ecclesiastical causes from civil intervention. But Milton goes even farther. He does more than bring them together: he makes them synonymous. One cannot be a true Protestant holding to Christian liberty if one's publications require an imprimatur.

In its very nationhood England was reformist; consequently if it fails to persist in the actions of reform it will cease to be a nation. As Rousseau will rebuke the elders of Geneva so Milton rebukes his cohorts for halting if not reversing the course of their spiritual revolution. Both Rousseau and Milton were sons of the Reformation, who from within the depths of a spiritual Protestantism, were able to chastise their elders for regressing on Protestantism's basic principles. By requiring that a book be licensed before publication, are not the new Protestants doing that which Luther accused Erasmus of doing: reinstating the rule of Catholicism? Licensing was required by the censorship prevailing in Spain. To submit one's free will and conscience to external judges is Catholicism all over again. Christian liberty is like a fortress in the soul; it cannot be compelled or forced, any form of compulsion defeats its very purpose which is dependent upon "inner persuasion." One cannot surrender one's inner being or set up another as judge of one's own conscience. The State, its magistrates, thus commit an assault on religion itself when they attempt to force conscience, which only produces hypocrisy or mere lip-service. The beliefs of the individual soul, grounded in the essential text, Holy Scripture, and illuminated by the Holy Spirit (by which must be meant the absence of ulterior motives or of petty arguments, soiled hands, a lack of readiness) stand inviolate against the powers of darkness. It is a reading imbued with the Holy Spirit. And thus we are in the original world of *Paradise Regained*. In his *Profession de foi* the Savoyard vicar in *Emile* maintains that no one can manage the elements of another's own soul, no one can "realize" another's own soul. One can see why Milton, like Rousseau, but more than a hundred years earlier, could maintain that Christian liberty and civil liberty (despite their separate dispensations) are intricately entwined. To revoke the latter is to reimpose the structure of belief against which the first Protestants rebelled. What was a religious concept – Christian liberty – could not remain within that dimension but had an expansive power extending to many aspects of civil liberties. These several parts are brought together in a concise description in *The Tenure of Kings and Magistrates* (1649), where Milton urges the people to "harken with erected minds to the voice of our supreme Magistracy calling us to liberty and the flourishing deeds of a reformed Common-wealth" (370). Minds that are upstanding, pervaded with the sense of Christian liberty, are able to hear (but more than hear, to heed) the voice of divine principle that works to establish true liberty in a polity. It is in this way that the doctrines of liberty expounded in the Enlightenment have their origins in the Reformation. But Milton's fear is that the Reformation itself was becoming ossified – and the introduction of licensing would be one indicator that this was so. Writing when the ideals of the Reformation were slipping away, his aim was to reform the Reformation, to show that reform is an unending project; it was for this reason he chose to expand the philosophical, moral, and practical arguments demonstrating why licensing represented a betrayal. Imagine what he would have thought of Coleridge having to pay for a license and for the stamped paper in order to publish *The Friend.*

Licensing itself is offensive to the native intellectual curiosity and genius of the English people of whom Milton is so proud. There is a constant source of renewal in the English mind (324–5), the capacity to overcome degeneration and "fatal decay" – an undoubted reference to Catholic Italy and Spain. For this reason the English do not need licensing but can be trusted to work their way to the truth through argumentation and debate. This position is revived Erasmianism, perhaps itself developed when that thinker came under the influence of the Oxford reformers. Practically, licensing is ineffective. If one has twenty censors (there were actually 34) one can have a multitude of different opinions. Then, there is the question of competency. Can this new caste of judges really come to a decision regarding a work that may have taken its author, through the most diligent labour, years to complete? Then again, how many bad books may have some buried gem which a cursory reading could not detect? Would the censors not be obliged to page through older texts for fear that some modern heresy enter under cover of antiquity? Again and again Milton draws out the errors of the Inquisition.

It is in the nature of human variability that some partial truths may emerge in delinquent texts: even schismatics must be endured for the spoonful of medicine that may be extracted from the bottle of bile. What is new may be unfamiliar but not threatening; threatening, but not incurable. To the modern mind, to the modern spirit, these qualities all helped create a buoyancy, a willingness to examine and to endure change. This explains how the basis in Christian doctrine helped advance the new attitude towards change itself. The attitudes of mind that created the temper of the Northern states may have their sources in this openness to new experience. And in contrast, as we find the concept of Christian liberty and its derivatives shrivelled in the countries of the South, particularly in Italy and Spain, so we find the spirit of engagement and advancement thwarted. The tenuous nature of Protestantism itself only makes more abhorrent the threatening powers of the Inquisition. Like the Index of Prohibited Books, the Inquisition is an instrument for religious control of secular policies. Twinned purposes for twinned agencies. But one should remember that the stern defence of civil liberties had its origins in the Christian liberty of the Reformation. The very principles at the base of the separation from Rome are invoked to protect the advancements made by Protestants.

Both works – the *Areopagitica* and the *Civil Power* – are major, each showing the prevalence of Christian liberty in Milton's thought. It is the fundamental principle. (See also chapter XXV11 of *De Doctrina Christiana*.) The earlier work argues against licensing and the latter opposes any projected attempts by a Presbyterian-controlled parliament to restrict religious liberties and to further dissuade the Congregationalists from any maneuvres in that direction. The *Civil Power* is written in defence of the plethora of new churches that found sufficiently safe harbor in England (444–5) – hence Voltaire's witty defence of safety in numbers. But the *Areopagitica* has a greater philosophical profundity and variety. Licensing, practically ineffectual and insulting, is, more importantly, offensive to the nature of truth and to humankind's quest for better ways of understanding. It is in these pages that Milton's light shines most brightly when he explains how shadowed is human vision, how beset by error and evil, and yet how great is the need for full engagement with the vices of the world. To know them is to despise them, and this is a major reason for disallowing licensing. Good and evil are so intertwined that one must face the worst in order to extract the good. The "doom" that Adam fell into was the plight of knowing good by evil (287). People cannot be cordoned off from the presence of evil. Nor should they be. "I cannot praise a fugitive and cloistered virtue, unexercis'd and unbreath'd, that never sallies out and sees her adversary, but slinks out of the race where the immortal garland is to be run for, not without dust and heat" (287–8). This most remembered of Milton's prose will be replayed again in crucial circumstances, even when the freedoms of the First Amendment of the US Constitution are being contested. People must be trusted to separate the wheat from the tares. Adult citizens should not need mentors who choose or read their books for them. Even Utopian expectations will not leave the world better off, "but to ordain wisely as in this world of evil, in the midst whereof God hath placed us unavoidably" (295). This magnificent sentence places humankind "unavoidably" in the world where evil is everywhere and humankind is immersed in it. The shadow of *Paradise Lost* is already making itself felt in the *Areopagitica* – perhaps not articulating the full-bodied sin and pain which are the burdens of history, the consciousness of which Adam and Eve must carry as they are expelled from Paradise (and which are proleptically presented in Books XI and XII), but still endorsing the acceptance of the world with all of its infirmities and faulty understandings, and cautioning against any requirement of purity or perfection that does not take into full consideration the nature of that world. In the midst of this treatise come premonitions of a world that Milton has not yet fully experienced, but which he was fated to more fully experience. The burdens of history are born in the history of the family, as parents see themselves responsible for the defects of children. Their children embody the world that they have created, only adding their own particular habits to the degradation of the race. On and on it goes, a practically insurmountable taint of original sin.

The practice of licensing implies that truth has been attained and on this false premise strives to protect the people from hideous evils. But these are impossible tasks. Quoting Proverbs, Milton compares truth to a "streaming fountain: if her waters flow not in a perpetual progression, they sicken into a muddy conformity and tradition" (310). His Reformation is in constant need of change and renewal: "and whoever thinks that we have pitched our tent here, and have attained to the prospect of Reformation … he is yet far short of the Truth" (316). Truth, once mythically whole, has been crumbled into a thousand pieces. Hence Truth is not attained, let alone enforced, but approached on humble feet. To each may be allotted some crumbs. Only God sees Truth whole and of a piece, while mortals are granted the beams of truths only by degrees. A brand of Christian scepticism that Erika Rummel has located in Erasmus finds its way through English channels to Milton as well.

To return to the choice quotation from Robert Bellah which serves as the epigraph to this book and comes close to summarizing its major theme, religious development is indeed the great avenue of change in the early modern world, and in particular, Christian liberty in Milton's thought extends its boundaries to influence the development of civil liberties, e.g., seeking to banish licensing, and affecting other strictly political concerns. This body of thought cannot be contained within itself but must, due to its very nature, the spirit of freedom, bridge over into the secular. The nature of religious belief must also undergo alteration, an excellent example of which would be John Locke's underappreciated essay on *The Reasonableness of Christianity*. This masterful treatise explains and illustrates the great landshift of Christian beliefs into doctrines that are more compatible with the coming Enlightenment (indeed below we shall show the proximity of Locke's *Treatise on Toleration* to Voltaire's great essay on the subject).

Locke locates the genius of Christianity in the method and style of the Gospels, which do not proceed with vigorous scholastic deductions, but with sayings and parables that appeal to the common understanding of the people. Locke begins by discarding the more drastic tenets of traditional Christian belief. He does so in accordance with his preferred companionable Christianity. The mild-mannered, gentle Locke wonders how a "felony" could lead to "an eternal life in misery," a "perpetual exquisite torment" (*The Reasonableness* 26). Could anyone, so used, believe he was: "fairly dealt with?" Can a "worthy man," much less "the Righteous God" inflict such penalties on humans based upon the conviction that all their actions are deformed and sinful and thus are subject to wrath (27)? And that the posterity of Adam be punished for his sin, the innocent for the guilty – how does such disproportion coincide with the justness and goodness of God (27)? By Locke's time such questioning had become if not conventional at least familiar. But what is taking shape is a body of values that has acquired some purchase attesting to the validity of human judgment, asserting that one can bring biblical lore before the bar of humane values, requiring that one be "fairly dealt with," and that the Deity itself meet the standards of justice and goodness, the values of a "worthy man." A new basis of judgment becomes central, strengthening the hand that Erasmus had played only with some ambivalence. Any radical change in judgment must enlist a new panel of judges with new casebooks of values.

Locke sketches a composite morale that appeals to the man of the world, the practical man, an ethic leavened with the "general golden rule" of Matthew 8:12. He then extracts from the words of Christ practices and prohibitions that enjoy a universal appeal. Christ not only forbids actual "uncleanness" (a spotless word for a host of lascivious activities), but all "irregular desires." I won't enumerate all the specific irregulars, but they include "causeless divorces, swearing in conversation as well as forswearing in judgments; revenge, retaliation; ostentation in prayer and alms-giving etc." These "irregulars" are offset by values such as forgiveness, liberality, compassion, etc. (*The Reasonableness* 48). While not exactly Benjamin Franklin's schedule of virtues, nevertheless Locke is selecting aspects of Christianity, as having appeal for the stability of mind and the flexibility of conduct that will typify the Enlightenment. Christianity may thus also be connected with the rest of the world, projecting (Locke would believe) a shared universal morality. Other people may never have heard of Jesus, nor savored the dogmas of the Church, but they can in their own ways participate in its renewed morality. The final reasonableness of Christianity consists in its capacity at home to reduce the tensions of faith and works, and its potential abroad to uphold the commonly shared patterns of a universal morality.

Milton and Locke were separated not only by a generation, but by a world of dramatic interest. Milton, the last of the Renaissance poets, was a full partner in that great cycle of classics of the modern world that began with Dante, while Locke was the originator of a philosophy that according to Voltaire consigned all prior approaches to the junk pile of history. John Locke wrote his *Letter on Toleration* in 1685 while exiled in Holland with his patron Lord Shaftesbury, to whom he was a confidential secretary, but it was not published until 1689, some thirty years after *Civil Power*. By the time of its publication, a formula had been arrived at that secured the independence of Christian and religious liberties from any encroachments of the State. Both works, *Civil Power* and the *Letter on Toleration*, were on their way to warranting civil liberties as well. There is a general pattern of similar argument in Milton's work and in Locke's *Letter*. English Protestant writers, whether concerned with liberty or tolerance, came up with an impregnable formula for distinguishing the functions of religion and the Church from the duties of the State, or magistrate. "All the life and power of true religion consists in the inward and full persuasion of the mind; and faith is not faith without believing" (*Letter on Toleration* 18). In fact, so firmly entrenched is this conviction that it anticipates the expression from Rousseau that Cassirer considers the central principle of Protestantism (both quoted above), "For no man can, if he would, conform his faith to the dictates of another" (18). A basic wall of inviolable principle surrounds religious belief which no force or compulsion can penetrate; once subjected to external control it ceases to be religion. The state's function is to "give laws, receive obedience, and to compel with the sword" (19). Humankind's civil interests pertain to "the things of this world, and not to "the world to come." From this essential difference flow the limitations on State and Church. The magistrate's power depends upon obedience, penalties, and compulsion – all possible violations of that inner persuasion. The individual may freely associate himself with a Church, but is also free to abandon that Church when it no longer represents his true beliefs. In cases of obduracy, the Church may excommunicate (an ordinary weapon but a faulty one at that). The point of Locke's ecclesiology is to reduce as much as possible the central beliefs "to such things, and to such things only, as the Holy Spirit has in the Holy Scripture declared, in express words, to be necessary for salvation" (21). Yet even with highly speculative articles of faith (to which Locke does not subscribe) it is not the role of the magistrate to suppress them: "the business of laws is not to provide for the truth of opinions, but for the safety and security of the commonwealth ..." (41). Locke allows for things that are "indifferent," traditions and practices not essential to salvation, but he also warns that once a practice enters into common belief it ceases to be indifferent.

Not one of these points is unusual – in fact, Locke had been working on these questions from at least 1660 on, and moved from a position of limited tolerance to one of broader acceptance (Gough 57, in Horton and Mendus) – once the essential principle of the inviolability of the believer's "inner persuasion" is established. To be forced to believe is not to believe. There exists a fundamental contradiction between oppression and belief. Maurice Cranston finds that it is the reasonableness of Locke's nature that sets his opinions apart from the harsher views of human nature and the human condition held by Hobbes or Calvin – the latter's God in his *Institutes* is still the God of wrath. "In the end reason was bound to prevail over passion" (in Horton and Mendus 95). Thus Cranston perceives in Locke's manner the spreading appeal of the Enlightenment.[1] In the thirty-year period, England has come closer to the Enlightenment, to be the country that Voltaire (from his two-year stay in 1726–8) praised so fulsomely. Christian liberty, its function having been fulfilled, has given place to civil liberties, to the protection of both the individual conscience and religious liberties. The way has been made clear, and Thought, in the Hegelian sense, is ready to stand without supporting braces.

The Outposts of John Stuart Mill

A significant addition to this abbreviated catalogue of the very germane transformations of Christian liberty, one of the fruits of the Reformation, is John Stuart Mill's *On Liberty* (1859). John Stuart Mill is a bridge figure of wide expanse, reaching back for standards of belief to the still vibrant Protestant past and extending his scope and influence well into the twentieth century. George Kateb, in a sensitive essay, praises the uniqueness of *On Liberty*: "There is no book written in English like [it]. There was none like it before; there has been none like it since."[2] Indeed, it is unique, but that glowing endorsement is given even greater illumination when Mill's masterpiece is placed alongside preceding arguments and future developments, helping to reveal the twists and turns that attend his thought. In my discussion of Mill I take for granted that there is no need for further expatiation on "the basic writings," i.e., utilitarianism, and feminism. Here we are adjusting the lens for a different optic, attempting to recover some equally worthy associations.

Scepticism has enjoyed a lively intellectual engagement with Christian liberty and tolerance. In Luther's full-throated assertion of Christian liberty there is no room for scepticism – "The Holy Ghost is no skeptic," he intones – while Erasmus will later regret his earlier endorsement of Christian liberty and would most willingly embrace scepticism if Holy Church would permit it. This gives some indication of future directions, where scepticism would only grow in importance and intellectual appeal and forge stronger links with liberty (less a Christian liberty) and tolerance. But there are risks, as scepticism may also have an adverse effect, one feared by both Luther and Rousseau, when by virtue of its alliance with tolerance it becomes the opponent of any inner persuasion.

In his defence of liberty of belief, Mill follows most closely and fully a single line of thought that can readily be identified with Protestantism, that echoes Erasmus's as well as Locke's preferences for debate and discussion, shares the clear-sighted ardor of Luther, and adopts Milton's arguments of a native son against "infallibility" – which was not officially made a Church dogma until 1870, though commonly accepted as a necessary spiritual aid bestowed on Peter and his successor vicars. But a very large caveat must be issued: nowhere in *On Liberty*, is there anything like the religious passion of Milton or even the gentlemanly acceptance of Christianity found in Locke. For Locke, Christianity, well watered down or brought up to date, still possesses some validity, and in its reasonableness is of universal appeal. For Mill, Christianity also occupies a large historical stage but only as one actor among others; its being is strictly historical with no penetration of belief; its ethic shows historical dependency, benefiting from what preceded it in Greek and Roman thought; its theological morality emerges from the Middle Ages and was simplified by the Reformation, but not to the extent the actual reformers believed (hence Voltaire relishing the task of completing the salvage work left *imparfait* by reformer fathers). By Mill's time, in his view, the various versions of Christianity possess only a portion of the truth, and when adopted as an educational tool or model to follow, may result in servility to "the Supreme will" but they are incapable of transmitting understanding of "the Supreme goodness." The language of such higher speculation stands out as unusual in Mill, resembling as it does that of Matthew Arnold. In short, Christianity, like all beliefs, needs to be perceived as representing an imperfect state of the human mind requiring a diversity of opinions in order to correct its own imbalances. Its import is mainly, even solely, historical (113–17). Without belief, Christianity, or any religion, is controlled by a historicism that of necessity enlists a multitude of diverse views, the validity of any one being limited to only a moment in time.

Not only individual religions but whole eras can be in error, witness the fates of Socrates and Jesus. And that worthiest of men, Marcus Aurelius, according to Mill a better Christian than any of the Christian sovereigns, a pagan who even gave better expression to the Christian ideal, stooped to persecution of the Christians. If the best can thus be tainted how about the worst (96)? Opportunity for error awaits at every turn.

Where, then, and how can truth be found? Mill's argument, like that of Milton, finds sustenance in doctrines that were once deemed heretical, but which later were found to be acceptable (his use of the example of the Hussites and the teachings of John Hus in England is prominent). One can learn much from heresies: the most important lesson being the challenges they bring to one's own beliefs at the level of basic assumptions, forcing one to assess again "the ground of one's own opinion" (103). He even finds value in "negative logic," that intellectual position which only criticizes without contributing anything "positive" to the argument (the Philistine reproach). The failure of Christianity to advance beyond the boundaries of Europe that it had attained in the first two centuries of its existence may be attributable to the tenacity of doctrine, as well as other unattractive features (a negative "thou shalt not" focus rather than a positive "thou shalt"; a passive obedience rather than an active curiosity). The errors of religion count for much in the development of Mill's tendency towards scepticism.

Mill belongs to an English tradition, one that he has inherited and expanded. Inhabiting it all is a critical scepticism, first launched by Erasmus, absorbed by Milton, and continued by Mill. The first step is thus the dismissal of any notion of certitude. Only the Papal chair uses infallibility to prop up its arguments. Error is widespread, even epochal. It is interesting to note in this study of the supremacy of the North that one of its commanding features is the suspicion of great systems of knowledge, which fly too high and thus miss the more direct and immediate access to knowing. We only possess our small, changing, and scattered measures of truth, nothing like the large complete totality. But this is not its only striking feature.

The influence of Mill and of Milton's *Areopagitica* jumped the Atlantic and played a critical role in the belated expansion of one of the great liberties of the American constitution, the First Amendment. Both Milton, with the founding principles of Protestantism, and Mill, who transforms those very principles, are present in the new life given the First Amendment in the years of agitation after the end of the First World War. In a splendid study, crisply written and sharply argued, Thomas Healy shows the influence of Learned Hand, Harold Laski, Louis Brandeis, and before them and through them Mill and Milton, on the changing thought of Justice Oliver Wendell Holmes (Healy, *The Great Dissent*). The backgrounds of Christian liberty and tolerance emerge, with their arguments entwined. Healy summarizes Holmes's major points, one of which is the acknowledgment that human judgment is so splintered as to be at its root fallible. Even if only provisionally, some limits must be drawn if we are to act. This holds true for everything except free speech. Because of this essential starting point (thanks to Mill), free speech is required in order to test as fully as possible all alternative explanations before verifying as closely as possible one's own judgment. By an uncommon reversal, Protestantism's key failing, according to Erasmus's critique, that it suffered from a splintering effect, becomes the very means, when exploited to the fullest, for arriving at some semblance of truth, or at the very least, at a judgment that permits some form of action (Healy 206). Although Holmes and his allies represented the minority dissent in a losing case, they felt certain of their position. Holmes's opinions were uttered with such eloquence and confidence (recalling the "dynamism" attributed to the upholders of the Northern position) that the "future of free speech was changed forever" (5). From Milton to Mill to Oliver Wendell Holmes one can detect a willingness to encounter the fullness of life, to relish the contest, the debate. The arguments of freedom seem to call up an emotion such as Lincoln experienced when he foresaw a "new birth of freedom."

As a warrant for free speech, what I call the "fallibility theorem" – which seems to be prevalent in epochs, great individuals, former heresies, and even in those objecting to merely negative opinion – is fully justified. But as a road to rendering judgment it has its own potholes and deficiencies that should not be left unexamined. The survey of other viewpoints might be informative and even serve as a corrective. But then again it might not, and the inclusion of another viewpoint might serve to confuse, derail, or degrade the discussion rather than improve it. It is still left to each individual's original qualities of mind to assess the validities of alternative judgments. There is the remaining question of whether one has garnered all possible entries, or whether there are better ones to come. In the quest for aids to judgment the dependence on a gathering of various opinions can result in a "perpetual abeyance" and thus defeat the purpose for which it was intended. In short, there is no substitute for common sense, fairness of mind, rational procedure, strong principles, and a modicum of learning. In fact, does not this over-extension of the "fallibility theorem" betray what Cassirer has found to be the central principle of Protestantism? Rousseau's first duty for humans was to not rely on the judgment of others, nor to gainsay the powers of judgment entrusted to oneself. On one hand, the need for constant reform means one does not rest on one's laurels, but it can also leave people battle-scarred, as issues that are not worthy of support become evidence of one's adherence to strict principles.

To this enormous red flag, Mill himself does offer a counter-statement, and it is framed, significantly, in the context of a professor in front of his or her class. In "Civilization," an oft-reprinted essay, Mill addresses education as one of the cornerstones of a viable culture, of a commitment to the formation of great minds (144). Its object should be to promote individual intellectual power and the love of truth. In his revulsion from any "dogmatism" Mill encourages reference to the greatest quantity of differing opinions. Thus his fallibility theorem is at work. But the privileged position of the professor renders it incumbent upon him or her to find some opinions as true, or held so by them. "To abstain from this would be to nourish the worst intellectual habit of all, that of not finding, even not looking for, certainty in anything." It is the openness of the classroom that permits this quest for certainty, for the students are free to identify and to judge the professor's own belief from among the several interpretations given. They must also be encouraged to absorb and appropriate the arguments and the values of the books they read. The course of study has accomplished its purpose if they rise to the challenge.

Mill's intellectual encounter with the work of Alexis de Tocqueville ranks among the most potent and fructifying meetings of two minds in the history of thought. One could say that the influence went in one direction and that it was Mill who experienced the shock of recognition upon reading the two instalments of *Democracy in America*. This resulted in two monumental essays, in 1835 and in 1840, totaling fully one hundred pages, but which read in many ways as a reproduction of Tocqueville's thought, so plentiful and full are the quotations. Mill benefited enormously from this remarkable study of life in America; his own work was animated and elevated by the encounter. They were both poised in similar positions of political thought and experience. Both had had great hopes for the revolution of 1830 and both were disappointed by the success of the bourgeoisie[3] (who granted no extension of the suffrage), and the "failure" of the more radical and democratic movements (Hobsbawm, *The Age of Revolution* 110–19). Tocqueville had come to America to study the two most pressing topics of the coming era – the growing acceptance of democracy, and as in a living laboratory, its realization in America. However simply stated, his purpose was massive: "I did not study America just to satisfy curiosity ... I sought there lessons from which we might profit ... I selected there of all the peoples experiencing [revolution] that nation to which it has come in the fullest and most peaceful completion ... I admit that I saw in America more than America; it was the shape of democracy itself that I sought" (*Democracy in America*, 18–19).

Tocqueville made the voyage and the visit, which differed in purpose even while comparable in some ways to Voltaire's two-year semi-exile in England (1726–8). Voltaire's *Letters from England* was a brilliant introduction of English philosophers, writers (Shakespeare and Milton), government, and political liberties to France. The two men differ in that Voltaire is committed to setting forth examples of the greatness of England as a model for the French. His method is cultural while Tocqueville's is largely sociological and political, depicting the combined characteristics of the Americans as a living embodiment of the democratic changes that will be overtaking the aristocracy in France. Although the revolutions of 1830 had been only a qualified success, and they are embraced by Hobsbawm chiefly for their future effects, they did stand out as the major means of expansion of political thought and action throughout Europe between 1789 and 1848. Despite their disappointments, they did ignite the epochs of change and reform that Tocqueville developed into his major thesis. He sensed the end of the aristocratic epoch and the beginning of the democratic age; he writes about the American democratic revolution because it was successful – at least, an accomplished fact. He was determined to understand what were the springs of action in a democracy and how they were modified by the specific historical character of the Americans.

It was because of this aspect of Tocqueville's study that Mill's thought and main concerns owe much to *Democracy in America*. Tocqueville was struck by an anomaly in the American personality. In a society so close to the frontier, in characters so filled with bumptiousness, with the idea of the self-made man, and the improbable ability of pulling oneself up by one's own bootstraps, it turned out to be unexpectedly quite conventional. How did this come about? It may be attributed in part to the want of illustriousness and other deficiencies of taste and quality control – the positive possession of which Tocqueville associated with an aristocracy having the leisure and the taste to promote excellence. What was really lacking was the aristocratic sense of individuality, even eccentricity. Tocqueville was persuaded that the American male was held by invisible social chains, the chains of standard opinion. In this way what was typical of American society was "the tyranny of the majority," the incapacity of the model American character to think and to act according to the dictates of its own consciousness, a reluctance to go it alone. Despite its being a ready station for dissident Protestant refugees, there was something in the origins of American culture, in their developing situations, that alienated the newcomers from their essential beliefs. Alone against a new and somewhat hostile environment they acquired a sense of interdependency, of communal, mutual assistance. The need for doing good created a nation of compulsive do-gooders. This derived from the necessities of their primitive conditions. Just as they depended so greatly upon received assistance, so they accepted received opinion. The worse thing was to be "shunned." And more importantly, the instrument is the mass mind but the active agent is the leveling cultural ideal of equality. The original quest for freedom (the depository of Christian liberty) has succumbed to the social goal of a cohesive equality. The despotism of the majority exerts its centripetal pull thus preventing independence of thought and willed action, extending even to personal habits and ways of living. There is insufficient self-will motivating Americans in this age to seek out their own solutions. They may exhibit their genius in technological and political innovation but in their personal lives they are constrained. Even when there is the struggle to break free, that drive is suppressed, as might be the case of Dimmesdale in Hawthorne's very contemporaneous *Scarlet Letter*; Dimmesdale secretly bears his own scarlet letter of guilt, and yet cannot follow Hester into the wild unknown. Is a shadowing guilt the disowning factor in the suppression of the American's social independence?

It is this argument that attracts Mill to *Democracy in America* and which becomes paramount in *On Liberty*, as it is finally an intellectual and social liberty that Mill is most concerned with and it is that which failed to make its way into the mainstream of American social life. Mill's reading of Tocqueville is an act of appropriation, even one of extensive addition, like any intellectual recognition. Mill however, respectfully, even reverentially, registers a demurral to the thought of Tocqueville. The same symptoms that Tocqueville detects in America, Mill observes in the middle class of England. This convinces him that "equality" by itself is not a sufficient explanation, that the real determining factor is a mass, industrialized, commercial culture. England, an aristocratic society with a growing middle class, is developing the same submissiveness to the "despotism of the majority" that was functioning in America. The culture of non-conformity, of individuality, was succumbing to the invisible hand (one different from that meant by Adam Smith) of a social group controlled increasingly by the mass media. Through this point of dissent the way was opened to Mill's classic *On Liberty*.

Do we not come full circle here and find that the very progressive features, the advancing thought of the Northern countries, the Protestant countries, created a world that struggled against the basic original principles of Protestantism? And in the completion of this thought do we not confirm the true historical accuracy of Max Weber's thesis? The triumph of the buttoned down, industrious, and dutiful Protestant ethic in collaboration with the spirit of capitalism produced the person who may have benefited from the Protestant work ethic but not the Protestant spirit of freedom.

The quality of Mill's thought may be seen in his attitude towards Rousseau. Rousseau, a twice abjured reconverted Protestant, could exhibit a fearless individuality when as a social philosopher he ministered to the ailments of his society. The medicine that Rousseau applied to an aristocratic society would be the same, with the same principles, that Mill would apply to the forming mass society of his own and future times. When Mill defends individuality in action he reaches far back into essential tenets of Protestantism. So, too, when he addresses the entropic spread of mass society and the tyranny of opinion (not even that of a majority) he reaches a full hundred years into the future and touches the mid-twentieth century concerns of America and Europe. He is writing out of a culture of comfort and known certainties, where the Anglo-American-Dutch virtues enjoyed a growing admiration and imitation throughout the world, but he fears the precariousness, the wavering fragility of such self-assurance. Mill, the so-called progressive, is haunted by the pestilence of regression, by the thought that even advanced nations can succumb to governments that are oppressive (97). Barely sixty years into the future thugs will take over the "civilized" countries of Germany, Russia, and Italy. But it should be remembered that while they earned that cognomen, they did not perpetrate the prior horrors of the First World War, but were rather their opportunistic products. To push back the responsibility for the destruction of European culture and society to a more genteel group of blinkered protagonists would do nothing to assuage Mill's sense of horror. It would only aggravate the thought that the leaders of society could march their contemporaries – entire generations of the best and the brightest – blindly to their deaths. The difference is startling between the world he inhabited and the world he feared as possible. He feared the very crack-up of the hegemony of the North and the values upon which it was based – severe strains at least in this superiority were beginning to show themselves. He was taken with the very common nineteenth-century sense of living "on the eve," or like Matthew Arnold, "between two worlds/ one dead/ the other powerless to be born" ("Stanzas from the Grande Chartreuse" lines 85–6). Arnold is considerably less perspicacious than Mill when he does forecast the dawn of a new more fortunate age (lines 157–62). So too, like Turgenev and Dostoevsky, Mill anticipated a coming new age. But where the Russians thought it implied a coming greatness (they would have been horribly disillusioned), he feared the generalized loss of the freedoms that his own society and its forerunners had so heroically and carefully achieved; this is for him not a projection but rather an anticipated reality, one that was already revealing itself.

To properly understand Mill it is essential to see that while he wears two hats, occupies two positions, there remains the same mind with the same requirements at work (see Owen Feiss, "A Freedom Both Personal and Political" in Bromwich et al.). One part argues for and helps bring about the transformations of liberty and tolerance (prepared by Milton), and the other, equally germane to its protestant standards, dreads a kind of mass society and the threatening engulfment of individuality, lost not in the heat of battle but underwhelmed by a slowly spreading gelatinous conformity.

Mill employs the phrase "individuality" and not individualism, and that permits his thought to assume a position within the great line of figures that began with the Reformation. It is possible to establish a difference between the two terms. If individualism might be summarized by the motto, "Every man for himself," individuality could be taken to mean that every person is responsible for offering and holding to his/her own special mark in the social mix and nature of the times. Luther denies the right of any person to impose his opinion on any other person (*neque ullam hominem* – see p. 90 above). When it comes to salvation, Milton, in the same tradition, insists that every person assume his/her individual responsibility: "Every man shall bear his own burden" (*A Treatise of Civil Power* 445). Rousseau's formulation is often quoted: in returning to his own past, this recovery of essential Protestantism has the mark of a "genuine discovery." And even later, John Stuart Mill's propositions – more responsive to the needs of his own time – are also genuine discoveries, or recoveries of the essential central principle of Protestantism, ones that will carry forward with accumulating strength and under similar necessity into the twentieth century. In summary fashion, he attributes the superiority of Europe (and of the North of Europe) to its diversity of opinion and of character.

As a cultural philosopher, Mill's thought is directed more towards the disunity of a culture rather than towards its unity. In order for a society to flourish it needs an innovative force as well as one of consolidation, each in possession of its own truths and correctives which are also only partial truths of a limited historical validity. Again like a double-edged sword, one side, from over-use, can lapse into dullness. Consequently, they must be in constantly alternating ascendancies. The one side stands ready to correct and replace the precedence of the other – producing a rivalry that benefits society. A parallel but slightly different example derives from the role of Rousseau in the eighteenth century. Following the exemplary thoughts of Madame de Staël and possibly Coleridge, in a culture devoted to the virtues of civilization, the "paradoxes" of Rousseau landed like a "bombshell" exploding the assumptions of the time. It does not matter that the propositions upon which the reigning culture was based were closer to the truth; Rousseau added a necessary ingredient that they were lacking: the value of simple life in contrast to the deformities of a life based on artifice (95). As a thinker of his time, Mill, like Rousseau, whom he admires, is torn by paradox, or thoughts that seem to go in opposite directions. In the words of Feiss quoted above, he wears two hats. One is that of the unbeliever, who participates in the culture, sceptical, and widely tolerant, that defers finality of judgment; but like the heir of the Protestant tradition, he is dismayed at the entropic, mass society, and its absence of conviction. In these thoughts and unexpected references Mill shows himself to be a cultural critic of lasting insight.

This is even more the case when he turns from belief to actions. In this highly selective summary, prior essays were directed against specific acts, practices or ordinances; Luther and Erasmus invoked Christian liberty to diffuse the ordinances of the Church, to do away with the reliance on "works." Milton joined Christian liberty with civic liberties in his opposition to licensing prior to publication; Voltaire launched a fuller attack on the remnants of superstition and Rousseau chagrined the elders of Geneva by showing how far they had deviated from the bases of Protestantism in condemning him without a hearing. But Europe is in danger of losing these advantages. Where Hegel cheered their advent, Mill feared their imminent loss. As a social philosopher his great fear is that these hard-won advances would be lost by simple entropy, by the casual negligence of a mass, democratic, egalitarian, affluent, and growing technological society. Here Mill's complaint is not so much against immediate practices as it is against the tyranny of the majority, the ever advancing role of public opinion. This is even more insidious as one cannot vent outrage against palpable crimes or injustices for the enemy is shapeless, faceless, hidden but extraordinarily present, and moreover very *bien-pensant*, in fact imbued with a cheerful if senseless enthusiasm, an idiot happiness, which offers greater protection than any coat of armor. Teflon is their trope. This is the product of a mass society and mass society is an entropic society. There is no rooting out decades of miseducation, of faulty principles, of adhering to the menu of mass media. This is not merely a levelling process but an ever-accelerating downward trend.

He identifies and prescribes against a massive and growing problem of contemporary societies. Ortega referred to it as the rebellion of the masses. But Mill would not have needed instruction from Ortega; he presents a similar argument: the mass man like Caliban "has a new master, [got] a new man." Mill calls this rule from the bottom a greater novelty: "the mass do not take their opinions from dignitaries of Church and State, from ostensible leaders, or from books. Their thinking is done for them by men such as themselves, addressing them or speaking in their name, on the spur of the moment, through the newspapers" (130).This sheer snobbism will be repudiated by novelists such as Dickens and Elizabeth Gaskell. But imagine what Mill would think of our time when newspapers are the organs that protest against a falling literacy (although their content had been geared to the reading skills of an eighth-grader), against the onslaught of concentration-diffusing television, twittering, and come as you are e-mail. He may even have provided David Riesman with the title of his classic study, "At present individuals are now lost in the crowd" (130).

Riesman and his colleagues return the favour when they signal Mill's work as representing an "extraordinary foreshadowing of the problems facing the 'autonomous personality,' the would-be non-conformist faced with the dissipation of the older hostile prohibitions, and the newer and far more subtle barriers of public opinion." They then cite Sartre, de Beauvoir, Fromm, Ortega, and Bertrand Russell as resembling the philosophical outlook of Mill in "many important respects" (*The Lonely Crowd* 300–1).

Given his various intellectual positions, both retrospective and prospective, his embrace of the "fallibility theorem," his standing on individuality and its role in a mass society, his extensive arguments in favour of freedom of speech, and even his ultimate abandonment in practice of the line of Protestant thought upon which his individuality depends, it is perhaps legitimate to regard Mill as being the "last" of the great figures representing that vital Protestant belief. Two adjacent sentences in his *Autobiography* illustrate the double position he occupies. It was his father who taught him to take "the strongest interest in the Reformation, as the great and decisive contest against priestly tyranny for liberty of thought." Thus, he concludes, he is one of the few people in his country who has not had to throw off religious belief: he never had it to begin with (29).

Certainly there will be many others following him (as indicated above), but none as indebted to what went before, nor as representative of what was to come afterward. Of none of the listed cohorts either of the earlier English tradition or of the later international aggregation can this be said. He stands in the legacy of the Protestant Reformation, but also represents its dilution, its negation, its being reduced to a single principle, that of liberty itself. Yet he still remains its heir. In all likelihood, his concession to fallibility threatened the very prospects of the individuality he valued. By virtue of the need to seek out all available judgments in order to secure his own we can witness the reversal of the very Protestant tradition upon which he so clearly and obviously depends.

So it is in fixing on the "last," one chooses not necessarily the latest comer – to which there is no end – but the one who represents the farthest and best reaches both backwards and forwards in the completion of a singular line of thought. Mill is fully present and active within a tradition but he also registers the end of that tradition. Where the equally ambiguous first depends upon continuities, the last represents the ending of a cycle, a foreseeable termination. This may be regarded not so much as a deviation but rather an extension, as a nemesis grown from within its very processes. In its quest for freedom of speech, for all the means necessary to ascertain rightness, it is so bound by a sense of its own fallibility that it depends upon all available resources and in so doing weakens the role of individuality upon which its free-standing judgment is based. In dealing with mass society Mill makes good use of the individuality that he has inherited, while at the same time he alters its nature and its role. It no longer represents conviction, or assertion, but rather their absence. Belief must be rescued by any number of counter theories before it can be ascertained. One must seek outside and beyond the self before it can verify the self, and that it never can do. When do we come to the end point of their system? There is none.

One can also ask if this procedure does not play into the hands of mass society – the absence of individuality that Mill deplores. It seems to call for the artificial intelligence of some super computer to conjure up all available positions to be taken on a subject. Active judgment may still be obtained but by means of indirection. One has at last arrived at Computerized Man. One could say that with this transaction Erasmus, or Erasmianism, triumphs over Luther's faith as assertion.

That which is "last" may be superseded but only when the focus shifts to other principles and agendas. After the revolutions of 1830, Mill had a deep sympathy for Marxism and the arguments for socialism, with one serious exemption: he did not favour the state's appropriation of private property. Ever faithful to his argument of freedom, Mill could not tolerate the centralization of the powers of decision in a ruling body.

From an expanded cultural and ideal history the camera shifts to material history, where the new interests extend to labour, capital, factories, and their effects upon the environment. These are interests that were hardly ready for discussion from among the earlier writers of this study. Of that line Mill represents the last and the utmost just as Voltaire, whom we shall approach in the next chapter, represents the fullest and the foremost. When one has reached the end it is time to return for better understanding to the beginning.[4]

Chapter Nine

The Edict of Nantes, Toleration, and Voltaire

In its Reformation origins the debate over toleration involves the presence of a substantial and determined minority body under the governance of a much larger ruling majority. Bayle informs us that Catholics were far more numerous but that the Huguenots were a considerable body in their own right (*Fondements* II 347). The resolution of this recipe for conflict involved years if not decades of strife. France, earlier than most, was beset with this problem (although England in the sixteenth century began to encounter a similar situation, but not with the same belligerence). Traditionalists, regarding toleration as a weak-kneed act of indulgence, stemming from a lack of faith and conviction, worked to extirpate the minorities, and this led to the St Bartholomew Day's massacre (1572), during which throughout France thousands of Huguenots were dragged from their homes and slaughtered. One cannot imagine this savagery as purely intellectual, but rather as quite irrational. This brutal emotional short circuit, in which so many succumbed to so radical an alternative, can only be explained if somehow they felt a time-honoured way of life was threatened, and thus, personally challenged, their only recourse was to strike blindly at the source. Their attacks against the Huguenots were well coordinated; emotional fury does not exclude calculations.

But here the plotting backfired, serving only to make more acceptable the minimum of freedom granted to the Huguenot sect by the Edict of Nantes. So half-hearted were these concessions that the revocation of the Edict (1685) had already been anticipated and made possible by the treatment of the supposed beneficiaries of the Edict. It has been argued with some justification that the so-called French Magna Carta, the Edict of Nantes, actually hampered the rise of Protestantism in France, consigning it to a permanent minority status and preparing the way for its own revocation as the edict of Fontainebleau. While one cannot praise an illness for promoting its antidote (except in extracts for vaccination), the revocation itself helped create the vivid and ardent treatises in defence of tolerance. Thus in the course of its troubled history, toleration was tugged and stretched from many fronts: the anti-party, the concessionaires, and the vocal defenders. These last were inspired by the works of Pierre Bayle, Spinoza, John Locke, and Voltaire, thereby enlisting philosophers and philosophy to enrich the field of religion – an endeavour that might be considered as the essence of the Enlightenment.

But while invocations of Christian liberty grew more robust (particularly as it was transformed), tolerance was always hobbled by questionable motives and a lack of reliability – it does not always mean what it says. But there is another inherent limitation, if not deficiency, in tolerance. It deals in concessions, is condescending, whereby one superior power is persuaded to confer benefits upon an inferior party. It doles out care packages and does not deal with equalities. Resuming the argument from chapter 4 and anticipating the special arguments that follow below, Maurice Cranston can insist that tolerance is a "second best," but under certain circumstances it is one that should be retained and even cherished (in Horton and Mendus 78–9).

Judging from the outpouring of essays, books, and learned conferences that marked the fourth centenary of the Edict of Nantes (1598–1998) the Edict is still with us, alive and controversial, and its great importance may be seen in the new readings it has provoked. There are three areas in which this famous document issued under the signature of the great Henri IV has undergone revised thinking.

(1) There is hardly an eminent French scholar who today would see it as forerunner to the Revolution's *Declaration of the Rights of Man*, which revealingly enough seemed to be the refrain of the third centenary observance. Although the Edict might promote tolerance, it may also be read as a complex political statement, hammered out through five years of intense negotiations where the term "tolerance" is in short supply.

(2) It was fortunate in its timing. After close to forty years of civil strife, with eight outbreaks of war, followed by an equal number of edicts only the last of which endured, France was ready if only by virtue of war-weariness to come to some settlement. The edict (as revised

in 1599) has 95 articles, some quite remarkable in their specificity. It was also fortunate in its monarch, Henri IV, brilliant in mind and personality. The last Valois, Henri III, was assassinated, to be succeeded by the first Bourbon, who despite his several abjurations still owned some credit and prestige with the Huguenots, to whom he affectionately referred as *mes Huguenots*. It is doubtful that this agreement could have been reached without the presence of Henri IV. He was first among the *politiques*, and the *Édit* was a document fashioned by *politiques*, or by those committed to political formulations. Pierre Bayle quotes approvingly the words of the Archbishop of Bruges who declared that one must honour as king that person who succeeds to the throne "par le droit inviolable d'une succession légitime" without regard either to his religion or his *moeurs* (*Fondements* II 347).

(3) It sought an end to a political crisis, rather than a religious one. It was a rallying cry to citizenship and to the welfare of the polity. In fact, its very first article prohibits any reference in word or deed to the past times of troubles and their causes, while the second prohibits any personal attacks due to references to the past. The third protects the Ecclesiastics [Roman Church] from any disturbances during their services; in fact, the edicts called for a restoration of Catholic churches and properties acquired by the Protestants during the years of conflict. (Solange Deyon 15). The Protestants are now referred to as "la dite Religion prétendue reformée" (the so-called reformed religion). The third article also imposes restrictions on the Huguenot places of worship, a consequence of insertions by the *parlement* of Paris.

Some critics argue that rather than leading to the *Declaration* it facilitated the Revocation of the Edict of Nantes in 1685. It can be read as a significant wall in blocking the spread and growth of the Huguenot populace and confining the Huguenots to a minority role in French life. Huguenots never reached more than one or two million at the time out of a total population of eighteen million; their numbers seem to stabilize at about 10 per cent. Thus while a minority, it was a significant minority, particularly once its centres of strength were removed from the North to the South of France, historically a more hospitable environment for dissenting groups (Venard, *L'Acceptation* 30). This separation was another North/South divide but one quite different from that presented as the thesis of this study. If any reading of tolerance can be learned from the document it is the negative one of its time, where tolerance bears the French meaning *supporter*, that is, putting up with, or enduring what cannot be prevented.

But able critics have rallied against this revisionist reading. They point out that unlike the previous edicts this one lasted a goodly portion of its 85 years and brought the reprieve that was necessary for France to tap its marvellous resources – a land of agricultural riches – and to regain its international position. The Edict of Nantes restored the primacy of monarchical power in France, such that Henri IV made way for Louis XIV. But Louis XIV revoked the declaration that was supposed to be "perpetual and irrevocable" by arguing that the French Protestants no longer had need of it. In fact, he claims that a large part of the Huguenots had already become assimilated Catholics. This being the case, the document continues, in order to eliminate from memory all the troubles of the past, the edict of Nantes is revoked in all of its parts. Protestant churches are to be demolished and their adherents are forbidden to assemble for the practice of their religion. Given the harshness of the revocation it is no wonder that approximately 200,000 Huguenots left France (Garrisson 16; see below). This was in 1685, when John Locke wrote his *Letter on Tolerance* (first in Latin but not published until 1689) and Pierre Bayle his *De la Tolérance*, both affirming the rights of conscience. Thus the movement of liberty expanded in other countries, while suffering a setback in the country where it may be said to have originated. This may explain why the greater Revolution, at the head of many others, began in France.

There has been significant scholarly reassessment of the edicts (and their transformations) that preceded the Edict of Nantes. According to Solange Deyon (15), of the seven preceding *édits* in a period of 15 years (1562–77), three contain important articles that found their way into the Edict of Nantes. The edict of Amboise (1563) contains what would become articles 1 and 2 – the much-needed historical amnesia – and anticipates what would become an article (6) guaranteeing liberty of conscience; and Saint-Germain promises access to all positions and services of the State, including universities and hospitals. So fulsome was the expansion of liberties in the edict of Saint-Germain, dubbed *Janvier*, that it has been understood to be the *veritable père* of the Edict of Nantes. Such articles and documents clearly call for new juridical courts, provided by the edict of Poitiers. This was to be expected as litigiousness would abound; in response, thirty-seven of the articles of the Edict of Nantes are devoted to the establishment and jurisdictions of these new courts (Solange Deyon 16–17).

Despite these "anticipations" and "provisions" the edict of Nantes was laced with articles favourable to Roman Catholics and noxious for the Protestants. It partook of the same ambiguities that attended tolerance itself. If it is a concession, a gift, just as easily as it was given, so in time it may be rescinded. This is why that fervent spirit and great poet, Agrippa d'Aubigné regarded the edict of '98 as a betrayal on the part of Henri IV of his former comrades in arms, even of his own convictions (see Lestringant, *L'Édit de Nantes révisité* 19ff).

Still there were ameliorations and historically welcomed emergences and advantages. Janine Garrisson wisely signifies the benefits of the years of peace (troubled and short-lived as they were to be). After Nantes, Huguenots were able to live out their religion not as a series of combats and conquests but rather as a daily faith in a country that was pacified. Its newly won foundation under the law breathed a new energy into Protestantism: churches were built or rehabilitated (despite the provisions calling for their removal),[1] preaching continued instructing the faithful in the theology and ethic of Calvin, and intellectual life continued in the colloquies and synods. In the words of A. Dupront, from a pre-Edict time, a heresy had become a Church (quoted in Venard 25). But even beyond these developments, given all the years and edicts that preceded, despite all the complications, set-backs, and antagonisms, the edict of Nantes played an important historical role (however measured) in the movement towards the separation of Church and State, and the acknowledged division between what were the public and what the private areas of conduct (Garrisson 14–16).

There is more to be said about tolerance and its own stages of growth. In *Homage to Americans*, a book of essays remarkable for its accumulation of incisive and insightful arguments, Eva Brann quickly takes on tolerance: "tolerance is not my favorite virtue" (3), and then proceeds to dissect the deficiencies of tolerance as an intellectual and personal quality. Working off her thought and applying it to the condition of the Huguenots in France, it is evident that tolerance cannot work between two parties grossly unequal in strength. In such a context, tolerance is merely a concession, something that one puts up with or a gift that is bestowed upon a weaker party – begrudgingly. Instead of the term tolerance, Brann would substitute respect, but respect that is not automatic or instantaneous, a birthright; rather, it is an acknowledgment, after sufficient contact and involvement, of the positive qualities in a person or people with whom one disagrees, or even shares an enmity. Respect maintains a dignity of the self while bestowing the same on an antagonist. Each is independent, cognizant of worth in themselves and the other. "Respect is thus (1) an alternative to tolerance and

(2) the better one" (22). Thus it is not tolerance, a half-way virtue, a "second-best" (Cranston), but respect that arrives at an ideal similar to the goal of Christian liberty and that is intellectual justice, an honest admission of the virtues of an opponent.

Because tolerance touches on *la morale universelle*, its constant enemy is fanaticism, which carries sophisms in one hand and a dagger in the other. Tolerance acquires value when it is found in opposition. It is preferred by far to bigotry, prejudice, fanaticism, and self-inflation. Despite its many virtues, there are drawbacks to tolerance; in its very nature some ambiguity and limitations are evident. It borders on passivity or negativity, a live and let live approach to existence and may even border on scepticism, whether in practical matters or regarding metaphysical propositions. It exhibits some smugness as if it were exercising a privilege in granting rights to others. It seems to assume not only minority status but also some inferiority or ineptitude in the recipient of its beneficence, which one is then obliged to support or tolerate. It never brings into contact two equal parties, but calls for "acceptance" of the other. Its blindfold is not an indication of the impartiality of justice but rather of avoidance, the refusal to see the other as a claimant of equal justice, for whom the majority party is also an "other," perhaps itself in need of acceptance. A minority group remains a minority group – one not fit to work its own ways in the exercise of power. The tolerated party will always labour under a handicap, and thus subject, as it was in France, to being stripped of its privileges.

Despite its ambiguities and whatever its causes, tolerance is essential to Voltaire's thriving state (particularly when opposed to the rising tide of intolerance). That is, at certain times and under certain conditions, it serves a very useful function. It is not surprising, however, that in his discourse on the virtues of the North (as expressed in *La Princesse de Babylone*), working on a much broader canvas, Voltaire should even introduce another concept, a third virtue, that of openness, an active engagement more suited to his nature. It bespeaks an active energy as to the things of the world – a sense of eager expectation and willingness to embrace – that may be even more attractive than respect, which establishes limits and boundaries. Openness truly conjures up *médecins sans frontières*, as intellect knows no boundaries. Its purpose is to seek out the best, not protect the acceptable (or even unacceptable). Its positive goal leads to the nobler concept of the republic of letters.

One lesson to be derived from the study of Voltaire's thought and character is that whatever may be said, there is always more to say.

Respect is better allied with justice, both given and received. It deals more in reciprocities – with nobody patronized. A poor man with understanding can speak on an equal basis with an official. Respect begets an aura that enfolds both; each is justified. To employ another kind of language, tolerance establishes a subject-object relationship; respect a subject-subject, and openness also a subject-subject, but one where the object engaged is "joyfully embraced." What it deplores is the phrase "acceptance of the other," whereby reciprocity is demolished. This leaves open the question as to who is doing the accepting and who is the other. All action is one-way, as the person offering acceptance is in a privileged position and the other exists in bland anonymity. Why should the process not move in the other direction, that is, the other exerting the same rights of acceptance?

Voltaire's conception of openness is active on a larger stage and is the sure indication of a prosperous state: it fears no evil, but instead welcomes foreign contributions, ideas come from abroad. The greatest monarchs of his time were all national extroverts, attracting prominent people to their courts, sending representatives abroad to learn the newest and most inventive ways of commerce and industry. The true genius of Voltaire lies in the exercise of openness in his own life. It perseveres in the life of a nation, extending from the monarch to people in power, to lowly artisans. Openness makes it possible for the lowest skilled people to rise but also for the sluggish to fall behind. Voltaire believed that when a country shuts down its borders it closes its mind and blocks possibilities for growth. It will resort to concealing its ignorance behind a self-satisfied wall of pampered exclusivity. It will chase away its most energetic and talented intelligences who will transport their ambitions and skills to the benefit of other countries. The truth of this principle does not require the many twentieth-century examples as proof. Already counter-Reformation Italy and Spain pulled in their own borders, and as a sign of their pending backwardness and retrenchment, Erasmus became a closed book. Spaniards were permitted to study abroad only under restricted provisions. All intellectual adventure abroad was foreclosed.

The supreme model for such international exchange was Louis XIV who turned Versailles into the intellectual capital of Europe, offering subventions to attract the best European minds and to induce the French to travel.[2] One can contrast Versailles with El Escorial, Philip II's monastic-military religious citadel. Following the example of Louis, Peter and Catherine not only opened the West to Russians but also attracted Western intellectuals to their country. Frederick II, Voltaire's great hero-antagonist, cherished the same principles, establishing academies to bring to Potsdam the most celebrated luminaries of Europe.

The great states are not riddled by fear but instead invite a lively intercourse with all that is valuable and available from other countries. But it was not always this way. Many of the thriving states had to undergo their dark nights of terror and bloodshed. The baseline of Voltaire's sense of history lies in such a period of atrocity from which the grander states eventually emerged. The reading of *La Princesse* should be preceded by the *Histoire des Voyages de Scarmentado*. This journey surveys only a portion of Europe and everywhere finds horror and desolation. The period marked is roughly the years following 1600 – an historic low point for Voltaire. It is the Age of the Assassins, where regicide is openly advocated, indeed costing the life of Henri IV. On the large dramatic stage of European history there are alternating moments where one is plunged into darkness before emerging into the light. And the possibility always exists of slipping back into the darkness again. For Voltaire progress was not a given, but a conquest, and a fragile one at that.

Toleration did and does travel choppy waters. From the Edict of Nantes through Voltaire and beyond it has suffered from its own internal ambiguities and deficiencies as well as from tugs of war between opposed groups. But following Locke and Pierre Bayle, it seemed to gather strength, until it reached its apex with Voltaire, whose *Traité sur la Tolérance* represents a landmark in the acceptance of the term as well as in his own development – with it he acquired a new voice and a new audience. Given his open and engaging, lively nature, Voltaire had always projected an aura of tolerance. Moreover, he became aware of the material benefits tolerance brought to a society. During the two years Voltaire spent in England (1726–8), he acquired a life-long fascination with commerce and industry and his intellectual interests encompassed the wealth and poverty of nations. As described earlier (11–12 above), the northern states of Europe, from Russia to the United Kingdom, underwent extraordinary changes in stature and prosperity. What are the causes for such accumulation of wealth? For Voltaire, simple industry and commerce, while necessary, are not sufficient. His reasoning expanded to questions of government, to civil and religious liberties. Voltaire's greatest acquisition in England was the principle of tolerance and the connection between tolerance and prosperity. Do unto others ...; Or (inversely) do not do ... Economic success, opulence, depends upon a regularity of relationships, the basis of contracts. Sudden arbitrary suspensions of such reliability are bound to cause panic and even flight. People thus require some expectation of stability if they are to do business.

In mid-career Voltaire had undergone a change. This was not so much a change in ideas as it was a change in commitment, an early Sartrean "*engagement*." From his earliest period of study with the Jesuits at the *collège* Louis-le-Grand, to his earliest works, the highly successful first play, *Oedipe* and his epic poem *Henriad* (first called by the abjured *La Ligue*), to his periods of semi-exile in the United Provinces and England, Voltaire had been an adherent of tolerance. This represented nothing new in his life and manners, which could be called an "aesthetic of opposition." After the "*affaire* Calas" Voltaire with new political animus and conviction became the central force behind the doctrine of toleration. From being a man of letters – considered the first great French literary critic – Voltaire became the first social philosopher of Europe. This event ignited Voltaire's intellectual energies and gave a new direction to his thought. Voltaire had written copiously of the value of tolerance, but that was more in the form of a meditation. Now he invokes tolerance as a philosophical principle that justifies his new claim on action. While there are many leaves to its tree, the trunk of tolerance, its source of power, works to dissolve the animosities of civil wars, while intolerance covered the earth with carnage (*Mélanges* 580). Tolerance invites many different types of peoples and sects to live together, which can only contribute to the prosperity of a country. One of his favourite examples is always Pennsylvania and the harmony and prosperity introduced by the derided Quakers. Many sects living together reduces the possibility of conflict, while one state religion induces tyranny, and two parties cut-throat strife. It does not hurt that the so-called "heretical sects" would constantly complain of the payments made by the State to Rome: Voltaire actually computes the savings the abolition of the tax would have brought to the national treasury, concluding, that the dissidents were much more "*bons calculateurs que mauvais sujets*" (573). Voltaire also laments the loss of talented subjects to the benefit of other countries, and contemplates their welcomed return to their homeland, mindful of the fortunes they have accrued.

The first consideration that inflamed Voltaire and brought him to his new intellectual activism was the scandalous torture and murder of Jean Calas in 1762. Voltaire did not jump to protest, but rather did his homework, accumulated the evidence before pronouncing that this was a case of runaway mob psychology inflamed by religious fanaticism exceeding the boundaries of plausibility. It was physically impossible for Calas to have murdered his son when and why and how eight of the thirteen judges found him to be culpable. This was the Dreyfus affair of its day; its repercussions were felt throughout Europe. Writing with the language of authority, with the firmness of a moral directness, Voltaire addresses all of Europe (*Europe entière*) when he denounces this atrocity: "Le meurtre de Calas, commis dans Toulouse avec la glaive de la justice, le 9 mars 1762, est un des plus singuliers événements qui méritent l'attention de notre âge et de la postérité." This is language of the true intellectual, writing from a powerful conviction, grabbing by the throat the essential issue of his day, and proclaiming its far-reaching significance for the larger world and those to come.

There is an immediate context to Voltaire's intervention. The revocation of the Edict of Nantes in 1685 had unleashed a host of defenders of intolerance, as the logical expression of a firmly held faith. Moreover, the triple slogan of *une loi, une foi, un roi* meant that one could not have two states in one nation, especially two founded on divergent religious principles. When Voltaire came to write his *Traité sur la tolérance* there was ample reason for him to take up arms. The encyclopedists were under fire and the *Encyclopedia* eventually closed down. In his concern for personal safety there was also cause enough to utilize anonymity, to employ his usual cleverness in distributing the text and for his measures to be tactical and strategic. His treatise is filled with fatuous praise of people in high places, people whose assistance and support he would require. It is written with surprising moderation (as Voltaire would say, in writing of moderation one should be moderate). But there is a difference between such tactics and Voltaire's strategy. This is why some reliable *Voltairean* scholars have attached themselves to Voltaire's correspondence. That his thousands of letters actually add up to a "masterpiece" is a proposition difficult to prove. (See the claims of Nicholas Cronk (3) and Christiane Mervaud (153) in *The Cambridge Companion to Voltaire*.) But there is no question that using his many letters from 1762 to 1765 shows the genuine motivations of Voltaire, his true aims of instilling "indifference" in religious matters as the genuine basis for tolerance; and most important of all, his larger design to separate the powers of religion from the authority of the state. All of these issues emerge in the *Treatise on Tolerance* and help explain why the treatise, despite all its subterfuges and hidden agendas – or rather, because of them – became (with time) a rallying cry for the progressive fortunes of Europe, in fact, became with Milton's *Areopagitica* and Mill's *On Liberty* classic texts of the Western liberal tradition.

The *Treatise* is a medley of Voltaire's many styles and arguments. It is alive with issues of French culture and society, from before the Edict of Nantes up through contemporary defences of intolerance. It is rooted in the Calas affair and a search for the victim's vindication. Two additions to the treatise brought the argument up to date: the first in 1763 praising the remittance of authority in the case to the King's council, rather than the judges of Toulouse, and two years later the posthumous rehabilitation of Calas and the indemnification of his family. It shows Voltaire's great historical interests, including, surprisingly, his finding of no arguments in favour of intolerance in the Old and New Testaments (or at least his defence of both volumes from any such accusation). It is a summary of European culture and its object of address, for all its French connections, is "*Europe entière.*" Perhaps this is the Treatise's greatest accomplishment, that out of a small but cruel provincial misadventure it creates a historical and philosophical work of great cogency and relevancy, showing that one can at the same time possess the passion of a polemicist with the thoughtfulness of a philosopher.

Voltaire entertains the idea of a cohesive Europe, one that in the previous fifty years had undergone enormous change, making it amenable to greater actions of tolerance (576, 632). The *Treatise* contains Voltaire's deepest and most abiding principles, including his simple credo of love for one's neighbour and for God (637 – a message that somehow even with Voltaire's commitment does not escape being only a starting point as a social ethic). One of its final chapters contains a remarkable prayer to God (*Prière à Dieu*), the main arguments of which seem to be a kind of Christian scepticism, or reductionism: given the immensity of the world, how petty-seeming are most of the differences over which human "atoms" are willing to go to war. It ends with his most poetic, complex, and lyrical praise for the rare action of Calas's vindication. He is cognizant that this is an injustice against a single family, which nevertheless in the midst of a spring calm fell like a lightning bolt upon France. A true intellectual, Voltaire draws the ultimate significance from this provincial affair. As a small candle in a dark world it nevertheless radiates major principles of a larger conflict that, however dispersed, never seems to be gone for long.

Voltaire's confidence was bolstered by milieu, his circle of *philosophes* and above all the string of countries in the northern tier of Europe, countries like England and Holland, where Voltaire's ideas first took shape, and other countries where these ideas of religious and civil liberties were being introduced. They had become Voltaire's allies and co-respondents in the new holy war. Through their qualities in common he was able to lay out the social programs that contributed to the continuing progressive evolution of the North.

Reason and philosophy have made some headway, Voltaire senses, changing a Europe of barbarism into one of civility. The treatise is at its centre a call for and justification of the role of the intellectual in public life. His great faith – certainly not a program of progress – is that change can occur, particularly if reason and philosophy penetrate the chambers of the great. And this is what has happened in the France of his time. After the work of the bringers of reason (he mentions the work of eight and more of the modernizing intellectuals, including Bayle and Descartes – the names are limited to Frenchmen) France cannot be governed in the same way it had been, and superstitions such as geocentrism, or the denial of tidal movement as being dependent upon gravitational pull, and other tokens of popular belief (Voltaire would not be without humour in treating some of the superstitions of today) are laughed out of court by enlightened minds (632). Reason enlists its long-time companion, ridicule. Along with laughter Voltaire puts to work another ally – the waning effects of time, which means that the mind must change with the change of the times. *D'autres temps, d'autres soins* (576). The Huguenots of former times are not the Huguenots of today. The issues that once seemed so alarming no longer command the same strident attention. The last "fifty years" by Voltaire's counting has seen the slow but steady triumph of reason; and the issues that divided people have as much relevancy as would Aristotle's categories (582). We may be approaching the spiritual centre, when Voltaire writes that his time is one of "disgust," of "weariness" which he then hastily corrects, "or rather reason" which is the warrant of public peace. And indeed, these are two elements that inhabit the valuable but limited concept of tolerance. One must start at the point where one is (582). Intellectual alteration in conformity with the changing times has been a V*oltairean* principle of social action and readiness since *La mort de César*. César instructs Brutus (a highly principled disciple of the stern Cato), that when the *moeurs* of a country change it is necessary to alter the laws. "Les lois, Rome, l'Etat sont des noms superflus / Dans nos temps corrumpus, pleins de guerres civiles ..." (*Dualisms* 114). Abstract principle must be avoided when set against the massive and threatening changes of the current situation. It takes a greatness of mind and spirit to comprehend the changed conditions and to act accordingly. France and Europe are ready for tolerance, they are ready for what is already underway, and that is the "reign of reason."

A shadow falls over that phrase in our usage, for unlike Voltaire we can calculate the hundreds of millions of deaths that have been perpetrated in the name of abstract reason. It is both fortunate and unfortunate that Voltaire did not live to see the horrible consequences of this new "reason and philosophy." Fortunate in that he was spared the horror; unfortunate in that he was denied the possibility of disowning it, of pointing out that his *raison* involved reasonableness, while the new reason means rationality, a dogmatism, a reliance on adamantine first principles just as *farouche* as the fanaticism he unwaveringly opposed. His reason makes ample allowance for human scepticism, the unfathomable complexities of the world. No river runs straight. The sense of contradiction and contrast are major components of human understanding. The absolute logic of human rationality leads to absurdities, or worse, atrocities. The religious fanaticism that murdered Calas cannot be separated from the secular fanaticism that condemned millions. This is why Voltaire's *Traité sur la Tolérance* is so important; its message is universal, historically relevant to the *infâme* before the Revolution and equally so to the *infâmes* that followed it.

What puts the brakes on Voltaire's acceptance of an absolutist pure reason is the lingering scepticism of the man of the world. He is quite cognizant of the human deficiencies that impede higher hopes. He seems to be saying, Things are bad enough. Let's not make them worse with religious wars. In his magnificent *Prière à Dieu* he begs God's mercy on *"les erreurs attachées à notre nature"* so that normal human failings are not compounded by fanaticism. And he concedes that the plagues of war are *inévitable*, but let them not lead to horrors of mutual destruction, particularly in these brief moments of peace (638–9).

Chapter Ten

The Pending Revival of the South

Two very large developments provide the background for the re-emergence of the South as possessing an intellectual order of its own. Most apparent is the legacy left by the return of the old East-West polarity. It reminds the proponents of the South that the way the North was allowed to define the nature of the South duplicated the pattern that was argued in Edward Said's *Orientalism.*[1] The Southerners were charged with being sluggish, lazy, dilettantish, seeming to lack method, perseverance, attention to detail, and numerous other degraded qualities. These qualities were the direct opposite of the virtues that the Northerners attributed to themselves. But the revived East/West exchange reopened the map of the world, showing the Southerners that these virtues appropriated by the North were not the only virtues and that their "opposites" – if such there be – were not necessarily deficient.

The lingering aroma of Fascist Italy and ultra-right Spain and Portugal did not help the Southern cause. But as the North had moments of its own that were less than savory, neither was wholly innocent. A more helpful factor was the noble attempt by the European Union to bridge the gap between the North and the South. At long last, after nearly five centuries, during which the North versus the South was the ranking dichotomy, the European intellectual community saw fit to introduce countries from the South into the European union. The shocking turbulence of the Great Recession (with its extreme austerity measures) has temporarily placed this political community on hold. It also revives the divisions that tormented for so long the countries caught in the Great Divide. Despite the relapse and the gut-wrenching process, another ancillary benefit had been gained: the confidence on the part of the protagonists of the South had been buoyed by their reintegration into the mainstream of European political and economic life and thought from which they had long been severed.[2]

A new shuffle has been given to an old deck of cards. As it was with the great North/South divide, where the rise of some powers is accompanied by the decline of others, so here the change in offices is something of a two-step. Where the South has benefited from its identification with the new awareness of world literatures and their diverse values and ways of being, the North has suffered a demotion from within, and this at the hands of its ablest intellectuals, artists, and writers. The very qualities that had accounted for its steep rise in power and authority, its long-lasting hegemony, no longer seemed to suffice, as chapter 5 above indicates. From the influence of external forces the South discovered an ideology that restored to them their own voices, but it was from within that the North underwent what Camus has repeatedly called the "tragedy of the [European] intelligence." In chapter 8 this study suggests that the nemesis attending the growth of scepticism was not a deviation but rather a consequence of the spreading tendency in Anglo-American-German thought. Scepticism bred a need to seek out all possible alternative interpretations and thus betrayed the essential maxim of Rousseau and its endorsement by Cassirer. In Yeats's "The Second Coming," this centrifugal impulse is richly enunciated, "Things fall apart; the center cannot hold." There are many ways to account for and even to describe this mood of disintegration. One way – followed in this study – argues that the basic faith of Protestantism in individual judgment seemed to fall victim to the abhorrence of the Catholic doctrine of "infallibility." Their own "fallibility theorem" seemed to produce logically a "perpetual abeyance," an inability to establish their own thought and values. The very values upon which the Northern ascendancy had been built were being undermined by the failure to hold on to some truths. The western intellectual becomes a patchwork of scattered opinions and beliefs (to Nietzsche's great scorn and enmity) and later according to Camus's *Myth of Sisyphus* acquires an inability to say "No," to declare some conduct as being out of bounds. The moral and personal qualities that had determined the North's superiority were clearly being diminished.

The world does not stand still. The South, while having slipped from political, intellectual, and technological ascendancy, did not undergo a total eclipse but still continued to hold its appeal as a centre of art, the storehouse of high culture, in short, the place presenting to view the major aesthetic achievements from the classical world up through the Renaissance. It was a necessary place to visit and study on any Grand Tour (for a splendid snap shot of what Rome had to offer the English tourist of the eighteenth century, see Robert Hughes, *Rome* 310–23). Young men and women travelled to the South in order to complete their formation and culture (however, as Mead points out, there was little interest in going to Spain).[3] But so did eminent scholars. Its appeal to scholar and tourist alike was also to be found in the spontaneity and colour of its personal stimulation, the street-language and bravura of its people, which represented values in contrast to the more reserved virtues such as punctuality and propriety that typified the correctness and high-minded principles of the North.

But this is not enough. It is, as it were, beating them with their own stick, or, as Franco Cassano writes, "chaining" them to the North's (West's) representation of them, and thus denying them autonomy, maturity, or ability to rule [themselves] (*Southern Thought* xxxviii). In response to such a caricature, different voices representing the South have begun to be heard, and legitimately so. The uprising of the South combined with the self-questioning of the North produced an intellectual climate the reverse of that which had been in effect for centuries.

A number of contemporary works can be brought together because of the paths they follow and the problems they address, the countries (Italy certainly, but also Spain – the suffering bulwarks of the old South) that they represent and the solutions they offer. The argument we have been following has been like a single stream that now spreads out into a delta of reference. The routings of these studies are similar enough: each points to a renewal of Spanish or Italian culture, one that had been subdued but now is seeking release from the dominance of the North and doing so with new arguments. They are intent on reversing the progressive Eurocentrism that (for them) was laid out by Montesquieu and Hegel, and on responding to the charges of a triumphant modernity.

Michael Iarocci in *Properties of Modernity* raises the question as to why the interest in Hispanic studies was lacking in the heyday of Modernism; Roberto M. Dainotto, in *Europe (in Theory)*, examines to what extent the South served as a necessary if unconscious partner in a dialectic that provided the North with its identity, and recuperates the work and fame of Sicilian historian Michele Amari; and Gayle Rogers in *Modernism and the New Spain* resurrects the argument of the "two Spains." One of the acknowledged leaders of this renewed vitality in the literature of place is Franco Cassano, whose *Southern Thought* provides most of the underpinnings of this growing shift. While welcoming these recent entries into the discussion on cultural change, we should not neglect the long-standing intimate historical and literary attachment to the culture of the Midi of Robert Lafont. (See his *Le Sud ou l'Autre: La France et son Midi*.)[4]

The first two begin by outlining essential steps in the making of the Great Divide. They present the outcome of this struggle as establishing the basic social and intellectual structures of Europe up to and into the twentieth century. The modernity of Europe had been formed by classical Northern and Hegelian Protestantism (not to be left out are the interlocking bourgeois, scientific, and industrialized aspects of the North). Both scholars are particularly interested in the consequences of this Northern *triumph* for the South. In fact, all five contemporary writers protest against determining the qualities of the South according to the virtues of the North.

Iarocci's introductory chapter is entitled "The Struggle against the New," and follows the efforts on the part of the South to re-establish itself against the hegemony of the North. His interpretation may be reinterpreted as an examination of how it came about that bright American students in the 1950s and 1960s had very limited interest in Spanish literature and culture (a remarkable cultural shift, so different from the curricular demographics of recent times). Their natural inclinations were drawn to French, German, and Russian literature, as this was where the exciting intellectual developments and literary achievements of the late nineteenth and early twentieth centuries were waiting. These were the authors and the professors who had a drawing power that seemed to speak with a more modern vernacular. Iarocci attributes this avoidance of Spanish literature to the great division existing between North and South and between Protestant and Catholic. What had begun in the sixteenth century, developed in the eighteenth and nineteenth centuries, continued at ever-fuller force pedagogically in the first half of the twentieth century. I realize I am taking small liberties with Iarocci's text but it seems this is one of the pertinent relays towards which his arguments tend. Thus he demonstrates the ways that Spanish Romantic texts can yield more modern and contemporary readings, and need not be caught irretrievably in the bind of the Great Divide (see his chapters 2–4). When the tide began to turn ever so slightly under the influence of German Romantic aestheticism, the Spain that was recovered was medieval Romantic Spain, certainly not the fallen Spain that had once commanded Europe for nearly a century. Even the Spain that began to emerge was dim in contrast to the varieties of Romanticism that thrived throughout the northern countries of Europe. Thus Iarocci is obliged to return to Spanish Romanticism and demonstrate how some canonical works of that period could have been retrieved had their ways not been blocked by the lingering ascendancy of modernity. The question his work poses (at least in my adapted rereading of it) is far-reaching and critically necessary and his solution affords new ways of approaching important texts of Spanish Romanticism.

But as a critic with very similar interests I can wonder if the reason for the flagging of attention to things Spanish can be attributed to the elements derived from the Great Divide. I recall a course I took at Northwestern University in the spring of 1954 devoted to the twentieth-century European novel in which as a freshman I read Proust, Gide, Mann, Kafka, and Camus – a course of study that left its indelible mark on my interests. With the addition of Anglo-American writers and some modulations they could variously be called high Modernists. There was not a Spanish writer among them. Here the preceding arguments of this study do come back to serve a critical purpose. The high Modernists drew their sustenance from a discontent with modernity; they encountered the eclipse of the material bases of modernity, as delineated in chapter 5 where I discuss "the paradox of time." The anemic appeal of Spanish Romanticism may be attributed to its failure to anticipate the weakened schematic of the formerly potent modernity, whose very foundations had come under serious challenge. Modernism was opposed stylistically, ethically, and philosophically to the major points of modernity. What had been the new was no longer regarded as new.

Spanish writers could not transcend what was only on the verge of becoming part of their intellectual world. The avoidance of things Spanish by literate students in the 1950s and 1960s was not because of Spanish subordination to modernity but rather because of its inability to go beyond what was considered modern. Spanish writers were fighting with the wrong demon, one already passé. Their *modernismo* was an attempt to recapture the social and technical values of modernity that the Modernists had already abjured. They were inclined to adopt its arguments rather than dispute its weaknesses; hence they could not have assumed the same confident positions vis-à-vis their culture as did the Modernists. They could not have risen to the height of the times, to employ the Hegelian formulation adopted by Ortega.

Roberto Dainotto greatly expands on the genealogy of the Great Divide, seeing the dialectic of history as intrinsic to the definition of the West. It takes two to make an identity. I can propose that the identity of the West began to form when the Greeks defeated the Persians, as Yeats well understood in "The Statues," where he extols the artists who with passion and precision made the statuesque works that "put down / All Asiatic vague immensities" (322–3). The dialectic between Europe and Asia provides the "rhetorical unconscious" that persists when the East-West divide turns to one that is North/South. Tentatively, Dainotto writes, this change was centred in the eighteenth century with the works of Montesquieu and later Mme de Staël and Hegel. Eurocentrism properly begins when a modern theory of identity – identity "an internal dialectic of the same" (64) – takes shape, "when the non-Europe is internalized, when the South becomes the sufficient and indispensable *internal* Other …" (4).

Evidence is quite clear that the great division was already taking place well before the eighteenth century, and indeed given a confessional dimension by Botero (see above). John H. Elliott, in his *Europe Divided*, provides ample evidence of its strong stirrings at the end of the sixteenth century. But, more importantly, Dainotto argues that when Asia was no longer suitable as another self, as part of a dialectic, and the shift was underway from an East-West polarity to one of the North versus the South, Europe itself provided the means. The South slipped in conveniently to fill the slot vacated by an Asian force. But this theory does not explain why the change had to take place. It transforms the result into a cause. The Turks were beating at the gates of south-central Europe, and could have provided ammunition enough. To prove its superiority and achieve its identity the North evidently needed a whipping boy. On the larger psychic map the entity in question needs an "other" before it can become itself. But there must have been some explosiveness in the warfare and contention between North and South, something more than the "rhetorical unconscious" for the shift to have been made from East-West to North-South. The South in its own right must have possessed the potency to cause so dramatic a transfer. In fact there was no other equally potent force; the drama with the South was undertaken for solid reasons of difference and not because of a psychic need to fill the psychological requirement of a dialectic. They abided by the force of circumstances.

Given the possibilities – and making room for some consciousness – would it be truly ideal for the North to choose an opposite such as the South? Would they have included the dominating Spanish oppressors? Out of fear of the Spaniards, Queen Elizabeth hesitated painfully and proceeded cautiously before providing minimal aid to the beleaguered

Dutch. Would the Huguenots really have desired to meet head-on the Duke of Guise and his confederates who perpetrated the St Bartholomew Day's massacre? Would the Netherlanders have called down upon themselves the atrocities of the Duke of Alba? Would the North really have wanted or needed to define themselves by the Council of Trent, where a revivified Catholicism stopped the advance of Protestantism? Of course in controversy one does come across arguments that move one to better realizations. But when Milton wrote his *Areopagitica* this was not against the Catholic South that he was writing (although he did have some concern over the long term threats of an Inquisition – perhaps a better candidate for carrying the role of an internal psychic enemy and constant companion as such) but against the Presbyters and Congregationalists of his own party. Similarly Rousseau had to minister lessons in the meaning of Protestantism to the elders of Geneva. Given these considerations one would have hesitated at length before succumbing to an "unconscious" impulse.

If one needs opponents and controversy to define oneself there are any number of sources available and not only one chosen entry. So, too, "unconscious" requires a psychic unity, but the "North" was made up of many causes and many forces (as the above listing indicates). There is also the possibility that one has entered the fray because one has readily understood what one is fighting for. We come back to Adam Gopnik's interrogative: Are there any rules to this game? "Rhetorical unconscious" is in need of a few more specific arguments in its defence; the North was not required to supply the enmity they encountered in order to meet the psychological need for an "other."

The third of the contemporary studies also addresses the "new Spain" and opens up the long-standing argument of the "two Spains." The tenets and practices of Modernism were not always destined to be a dead letter in Spain. The savagery of the First World War prompted a renewed resolution to go beyond the nationalism that had unleashed the dogs of war. Spain, although neutral in the war, experienced a new internationalism. Its closed frontiers opened once again, led by the new journal *Revista de Occidente*, under the editorship of Ortega y Gasset. This journal was committed to publishing the best that could be had in Europe – and the backlog was enormous after war's end. It had a counterpart in Great Britain, *Criterion*, directed by T.S. Eliot. Thus, two of the leading intellectual lights of Europe were in similar positions, with similar aims and intentions. Even their relationship bordered on the symbiotic. Eliot had a ready and plausible goal in mind, namely, to expand the horizons of the implied insulated culture of Great Britain, a goal that was consistent with his poetic practice in *The Waste Land*.

What was most critical was the cooperation of the two journals in the spread of Modernism – this was the epoch when the banners were raised of the little mag. Eliot of course in his poetry and practical criticism was a leading Anglo-American modernist and Ortega contributed greatly as a theoretician, witness his *La Rebelión de las Masas* (brought out in our time in a splendid new edition by the late Thomas Mermall),[5] and its complementary work, *Il Tema de Nuestro Tiempo*, and essays on *perspectivismo*, or, the doctrine of the point of view, and relativity – the last, he was proud to say, before Einstein.[6] The seal on this relationship may have been set by Antonio Marichalar and his insightful and provocative essay, "James Joyce en su laberinto," appearing in the *Revista* in 1924. Marichalar was tireless in bringing not only Joyce to Spanish awareness but also many other figures of Modernism.[7]

This "new Spain" harkens back to another age of international brightness, of intellectual cooperation and cross-fertilization, to a republic of letters, when Erasmus was in close communication with the enlightened circle of English humanists, variously referred to as the Oxford, London, or Florence Reformers. With no journals to spread the news this was the time when letters, copious, abundant letters were regarded as essays and journal articles would be later. A letter from Erasmus was treated by its recipient as a precious commodity, to be shown off and admired for its Latin style and content. Although Latin was the lingua franca, the normal language of exchange between scholars, clerics, and officials (when they were about their business), translations of the mainly Greek classics were transformative, witness merely the works of Plato and Plutarch. And the central text was the Bible. Here Spain's circle of humanists, under the leadership of the great cardinal Cisneros, produced the Bible in its early Greek texts, in revised Latin, and even in Aramaic. Cardinal Cisneros may have been simply more astute with his finger to the wind when he perhaps allowed Erasmus's version of the new Bible, with Latin annotations, to appear first and thus be the object of attack. But unlike Erasmus he was a high churchman, who was naturally more conservative, and who did not correct Latin phrases with Greek, and whose delay may have been further caused by the seven linguistic versions he reproduced in his polyglot edition. By 1521 Erasmus's name became anathematized in Spain, after the advent of the Lutheran programs for reform, by virtue of being associated with the early Luther. Symbolic of the complete closing of the Spanish intellectual mind was the fact that by mid-century Erasmus was totally excluded (see Bataillon, Menchi, and Elliott).[8] The forces of darkness, the old Spain, always waiting in the wings, found their moment provided for them and brought closure to that early enlightened movement of Spanish humanism.

Spain and Great Britain enjoyed the intellectually rich years before the recommencement of the world wars of the twentieth century. But there were anomalies: under the soft dictatorship of Primo de Rivera the *Revista* continued its activities and Ortega became a leading advocate of the coming Republic. Yet, despite their continuing intellectual leadership, both Eliot and Ortega began to suffer some loss of prestige. Eliot professed his Christian faith, his politics as royalist, and his literary taste as classical (all of which were modified if not altered by the poetic realities of *Four Quartets*). Ortega, after his original enthusiasm, was put off by the extreme anti-clericalism of the Second Republic, and by its seeming repetition of the errors of nineteenth century liberalism. With the coming of Franco, Ortega found refuge abroad but in the eyes of former adulators and supporters lost a great deal of credit when he returned to live and work in Spain under Franco. Maria Zambrano particularly became disenchanted as she was one of the many Spaniards who accepted permanent exile as their lot (which, fortunately, did not last).

But their work had yielded results. Marichalar, imitating Lytton Strachey, introduced the vogue of ironic or even satiric biography. There are always reasons for the revivals of biography. In the United States the growth of postmodern interest in biography was in no small part a reaction against the influential vogue of theory. Something similar happened in Spain, as Ortega felt biography would bring literature back in touch with the circumstances of life. In a brief period from 1929 to 1936 over 300 biographies were reviewed in the newspaper *Sol* (Rogers 108–9). Under the veneer of biography elements hostile to the regime could be cleverly introduced. The republican Marichalar's life of the Duke Osuna in essence showed the destructive impact of the nineteenth century Spanish aristocracy.

The dark forces of war calling for blood sacrifice blighted the relatively brighter promise entertained by Modernism. For both Eliot and Ortega, their hopes for a new republic of letters were thwarted by Great Wars – but they were different wars: when Spaniards refer in conversation to the Great War they do not mean either of those two world wars, but rather their own calamity of 1936–9. Literary production continued in the Franco years, and predictably after him but with none of the promise and stature of the pre-war years, culminating in the so-called generation of 1927. Even post-Franco Spain was throttled and bruised at home. It did not live on the verge of promise, as it had in the years after the First World War, a period that had motivated Ortega and the internationalism of *Revista de Occidente*. With the coming of his war, Eliot, wrung through with humiliation, suspended publication of *Criterion*. Unlike his counterparts in Spain, however, Eliot went on to write some of the greatest poetry of the century in the English language, his *Four Quartets*. Perhaps hope and promise are not the *sine quae non* of creativity.

Dainotto devotes several valuable chapters to the nineteenth-century historian Michele Amari who describes the Sicilian Vespers (the uprising of the people of Sicily in 1282) as an essential step in the gradual triumph of freedom, serving as a programmatic template for the revolutions in Europe of the early nineteenth century. Rather than seeing it as a dynastic conflict, he regards that insurrection as a rebellion of the people. But this reading was misinterpreted by European historians, thus ignoring and even erasing five centuries of Southern history. Here there is no reference on Dainotto's part to "unconscious" replacements; nor is there the apparent endorsement of Montesquieu's preeminence in the middle of the eighteenth century, his central position in the consolidation of the deliverance of the North (see p. 194). Now Montesquieu is faulted for having helped establish the Northern predominance that results in the systematic exclusion of the South, the relegation of the South, in fact, to a position of subordination where it was undone by the very colourful habits of speech, the nonchalant dress, and character attributed to it by the North.

Both in Spain and in Italy the closeness of Africa was a desert to be avoided; from it only ill winds blow to infect the South of Europe. The desert is a kind of no-man's land. Lines had to be drawn not in the sand but rather in the South of those countries that front on Africa. If Aeschylus's *The Persians* symbolically separated the West from the East, Virgil's *Aeneid* defined Latin Europe by its separation from Africa. If there is an "unconscious" remnant it is by association with Africa. Thus the southern parts of France, Italy, and Spain are cordoned off in the popular imagination like islands belonging to Africa. For the French, south of Lyons is Africa; for the Italians, south of Naples is Africa, and for all of Spain, south of the Pyrenées is Africa. Africa does not begin at the water's end but rather in their lower backyard, the South, which accumulates almost as an inheritance the prejudices that attach to Africa. This is the very situation Cassano seeks to remedy by providing the South with its own words of self-discovery, to let the South define itself.

The task confronting the writers of the "Southern school" is to undo the "meridionalism" (similar to Orientalism) which understands the South by the categories the North provided for them. These qualities tend to be of high entertainment value, as colourful speech, music, and dance – not the qualities of a personal seriousness and intellectual attainments. It is for these reasons that Amari spent the latter part of his life (five volumes' worth) retrieving the role of Muslim culture in building the civilization of Europe (Dainotto 198–217).

In his leading role, Cassano means to emphasize the qualities of the South that might contribute to the better health of the North. The South brings moderation, which is not a balancing act – a pinch of this and of that, as in a recipe – but rather a modulation of basic principles, a need for an inner balance that defines the entire personality. This is not the place to summarize the refined points of *L'Homme révolté* but simply to indicate that in its essential arguments and in the section titled "Les pensées du Midi" Camus serves as model and confirmation, providing a glossary of terms, for what the new apologists were advocating. Camus is addressing "the error of a whole period of history" (*L'Homme révolté* 419), that period that cannot summon the resources to condemn the nihilism that accepts the murder of untold millions, that yields to the obliterating sands of the desert. But there is a difference in that Camus is attempting to separate himself and his theory from the history of his time, to effect a kind of moral separation. For instance, the line he draws between suicide and atrocity: suicide kills the self and spares the other; the new breed of rationalized murder, kills the other and spares the self. *Révolte,* by drawing a line, brings a correction to moral conduct, as when a slave rises up against maltreatment and opposes brutality, he acts for all humanity in declaring that there is a line of conduct that cannot be tolerated. It is the rock bottom repudiation of nihilism. But such *révolte* does not bestow an absolute liberty. The same moral action by which he claims his own liberty acts as a restraint against depriving another of his or her freedoms. Thus for Camus revolt brings a yes and a no together (686–9). There are no absolute prerogatives – neither of liberty nor of justice – but each measure is modified by its counter. The poisonous potion is excess (*démesure*), particularly in the twentieth century when a justifying historical rationalism is added to the mix.

The fixtures are given recognizable names and faces in a remarkable sub-section, also entitled "La pensée du Midi," where the combatants are arrayed in their proper North/South formations, with the conflict between the *"idéologie" allemande* and *"l'esprit méditerranéen"* (*Essais* 700–2) (an identification that Sartre ridicules in his riposte as being a gesture of personal tribalism). Camus lists the antinomies that "traduisent une fois de plus la longue confrontation entre la mesure et la démesure qui anime l'histoire de l'Occident ..." (702). This formulation, present even in the ancient world, recurs yet again in the divided thought of the twentieth century, and Camus leaves it as a legacy and support in moral philosophy for his followers who invoke the qualities represented by that great middle sea, the Mediterranean. Implicit in the Midi, as Camus argues in *L'Homme révolté*, is the sense of limits, the combination of opposing qualities that act as a brake on excess. One knows where to draw the line, indeed one knows when that line has been crossed. This is a warning not only at the end of an action, but an awareness before the act.

To be sure, modern thought has also exiled Helen and beauty, nature and its resources (see *"L'exil d'Hélène"* 813–17); its empire is built over a desert. Through the arguments of *l'Homme révolté*, the new apologists for the South found both comfort and confirmation. Cassano would slow down the pace of Northern man, described now as *homo currens*, man in a hurry, always rushing, and in this way is approaching the thought of Wordsworth, already prominent in English Romanticism. *Andante* is the mode of reflection and composition. The daily hustle disperses concentration, the real characteristic of intelligence that fixes on the nature of things.[9] A full dossier of prescriptions is assembled, to restore qualities with which the Modernists themselves would agree. If the South managed a remarkable shift in values so did the North. In challenging modernity the new Southerners were in some sense kicking at a half-opened door, as the greater intellectual tendencies of the North, the tendencies that were receptive to the advances of the South, were embodied in the new sensibilities of Modernism.

Quite obviously these new voices from the South are not in error, they are merely incomplete. It should be remembered that leading intellects of the North (or latterly, the West) had begun to issue their own warnings about the weaknesses threatening the make-up of the archetypal western man. Already in 1900 Thomas Mann in *Buddenbrooks* and Joseph Conrad in *Heart of Darkness* had shown the built-in tendencies to self-destruction. They took their examples from the heights of their culture. My own *Mapping Literary Modernism* (1985), confederate in some aspect with the works of Cassano and his associates, argued that the "paradox of time" produced the nemesis that awaits the full implementation of the unfettered time world derived from the Renaissance. The change in typology and sensibility, the avoidance of the linear, and the responsiveness to differing layers and areas of experience already fulfil the needs of the new world advocated by the old world of the South.

That the two can come together may be encapsulated in a classical spiritual "meeting" of Albert Camus and T.S. Eliot, hardly brothers under the skin. Albert Camus as Mediterranean man stands out as an exemplar for the new South. And Eliot as poet and critic stands out as the grand master of high modernism. The mediating figure was Simone Weil whom Camus so revered that he requested a private session with her as she lay dying in a French hospital. T.S. Eliot was deeply moved by the spiritual qualities of her works which were only published posthumously, beginning in 1948. Such triangulation indicates that there may be much to be gained by collusion between high Modernism and the recovered sentiments of the Midi.

Chapter Eleven

Towards a Summation

One of the purposes of this study has been to push the beginning of the Great Divide back to its rightful origins in the sixteenth century. Here once again matters of chronology serve a critical purpose: they establish the dramatic changes and continuities between the Renaissance-Reformation and the Enlightenment. The four critical concepts that are examined, rather than demonstrating supplantation or supersession, undergo a process of development. In their unfolding of powers that were always implicitly present they establish pathways from one period to another.

To reflect upon a book of reflections, the first effect one can gather from these changes is the entry into political life of religious freedom, most notably as Christian liberty. The quotation from Robert Bellah at the head of chapter 1 attests to this process. This did not hold true for the South, where we find verified the brilliant picture Mme de Staël draws of literature and philosophy themselves suffering from a lack of religious freedom. But it does hold true in the radicalization of the Reformist politics of the North, and most overtly in John Milton's mature completion of the marriage between Christian liberty and civil liberty. One cannot be a genuine heir of Protestantism, nor can one be true to one's English heritage if the free expression of thought is subjected to the prior censorship of a required imprimatur. One can already detect in Milton a germ of the notion that only would later come to the fore, the fear that once truth becomes a solidified attainment it runs the risk of defeating the Protestant principle of constant renewal (see Milton above, and Mill).

A second defining step in the development of the Great Divide is the entrance of philosophy into religious life. It was Voltaire's fondest dream that sectarianism would yield to a *morale universelle*. This was already Locke's great subject when he thought that in its "reasonableness" Christianity could have universal appeal. It was the philosophical spirit of the peoples of the North [*presque tous*] that led them to adopt Protestantism. Now, Mme de Staël writes, it is among the same Protestant countries that philosophy is allowed to grow without restraints. But her vision of *perfectibilité* is accompanied with a ground swell of challenge, one that haunts the established Protestant religions of the North. Will their supremacy bring with it a spiritual tyranny? She departs from her subject to ask enlightened thinkers whether it is possible to join *morale* with the idea of God, without this ideal combination then becoming an instrument of oppression. What should be the source of the greatest happiness among people, can also "every day" break the bonds between people that are based upon *la délicatesse, l'affection ou la bonté* (*De la littérature* 186–7). The marriage between religion and philosophy receives its greatest endorsement as well as its gravest caveat, in the name of those values that represent the true sensibility of the Enlightenment: delicate handling, affection, and goodness.

As the summary paragraphs above indicate, a work thrives upon anticipation, i.e., that it keep its earlier promise and its project be sustained and brought to completion. Yet the author welcomes the unanticipated surprises that are disclosed by the material itself. Some are indeed minor, the way, for instance, the four concepts so prominent in the text will team up, and enter into a partnership, such as Christian liberty with time. Others might be quite explosive. By far the most imposing unanticipated development occurred when the very genius of Protestantism seemed to turn against itself, and in its opposition to papal infallibility, its susceptibility to the theorem of fallibility, or the human disposition toward error, weakened its hold on some of its recognized principles. The "inner persuasion," the strength of personal conviction, the refusal to rely on the judgments of others – and underlying all, the need for faith – began to fade. Furthermore they found themselves foundering in the conclusion that truth was elusive and difficult to attain and sustain. Such a position could lead to an abeyance of judgment and the abandonment of the values that had led to the ascendancy of the North. They found themselves besieged by the same division in thought (the *Entzweiung*) that for Hegel characterized the Southern mentality in its inability to initiate a reformation. Just as the triumph of time turned into the triumph of space, so the full culling and cultivation of a multitude of possible ways of viewing any problem, leading to a superabundance of variables, can turn inner certainty dependent upon faith into a flood of evidence and information that only a computer can manage. The era of computerized man is upon us, and there is not a crucial area of our society – from baseball to Wall Street – that is not fragmented in its ways of acquiring knowledge, the kind of knowledge that leads to true judgment and right action.

Such developments extend the subject of this book into issues of contemporary life. Their import is conveyed well in another of those encompassing yet brief aphorisms of Yeats "The best lack all conviction/ While the worst are filled with passionate intensity." It is this situation that Albert Camus works to alleviate by bringing some possibility of truth into the tragedy of the European intelligence.

This might be the real basis of the resistance of the Southern countries to the advent of an aggressive Protestantism. This "new philosophy that calls all in doubt" may be regarded as depriving the group of a sense of completion, of a vision containing philosophical wholeness in the nature of things, of a picture of coherence and a sense of cohesiveness in one's existence or finally some continuity itself. Of course, it is so easy with this awareness to slip into decay and decadence, and to suffer the humiliation of being surpassed, or superseded (i.e., Richard II). To know when and what to change remains one of the constant challenges facing humankind. And it was at this fulcrum, this genuine divide, that the battle and battles of reform were and are constantly being fought. A need for the person to find cohesiveness in culture and thought is now confronted by doctrines of radical change abetted by the widening spread of scepticism. These differences and collisions locate the ongoing Reformation debate at the deepest levels of the needs of the human personality. The quest for permanence remains one of the essential purposes of religion, while the very question of some modicum of continuity pulls at the heart of much modern poetry and philosophy. The loss of a sense of continuity and of any kind of cohesion are the threatening slopes on which modern thought has been inclined. Perhaps each to differing degrees might fall short of Alfred North Whitehead's desideratum, that we ask of [poetry] "that it express that element in perishing lives which is undying by reason of its expressions of perfection proper to our finite natures" (Whitehead actually asks this of theology, *Adventure in Ideas* 176).

In chapter 8 I made much of the position of John Stuart Mill as the last in the series of thinkers whose notion of liberty has its origins in the Reformation while extending into the nineteenth century, with great anticipation (in Mill's case) of the twentieth. If anyone earned the right to be the "last," as a summary contributor to a single cycle of thought, it was Mill. To be last is not dusty or crepuscular, far from it (witness Mill's influence on the important but minority opinion of Oliver Wendell Holmes concerning the First Amendment). But as soon as we turn into the winds of the nineteenth century we see what has been missing. We have been covering – and rightly so – a kind of mixed history, a history of ideas, through the developments of four concepts, themselves immersed in changing cultures.

These concepts might seem to be ages away from the fuller realization of the North/South divide in the then-coming industrial revolution. Indeed, in Elizabeth Gaskell's *North and South* (1855), indications of change are enormous. The factory town of Milton (Manchester) experiences intense strife between management and the union. The waves of protesting violence are irrational, headstrong surges against authority, but they have nevertheless been provoked by management, importing strike-breaking Irish workers, called "knobsticks." This is only a part of the issues at work: Mrs Hale is dying of cancer, attributed to the foul city air; and Bessy Higgins dies of lung weakness caused by the fluff or the dust from the cotton gins. The temper of the time is so very different, demonstrated also by the growth of dissenting Peace Societies. Erasmus wrote the "*Querela pacis*," but had no conception of a collective society devoted to peace. The march of large segments of the population to the better-paying jobs of the North leaves behind in nostalgic reverie the idyllic villages of the South. And the fall of coal dust leaves smudges of grime everywhere. Yet black coal is gold.

Despite these staggering differences, continuities persist. One of the most striking is portrayed by the mill owner Mr Thornton, who expresses the cultural enjambement that this study emphasizes. Cromwell, he believes, would have "made a capital mill owner" (123). Patricia Ingham in her strenuously argued yet possibly narrow Introduction to the Penguin Classic *North and South*, regards this statement as little more than a joke. But Margaret Hale does not regard it as a joke and responds that Cromwell was never one of her heroes. Later it is explained that Thornton's lack of humour is notorious. This remarkable conjunction, joke or no joke, would later be validated by both Max Weber and David Landes (see above pp. 67–9). Despite their clashing but superficial political antagonisms, Margaret Hale rushes to Thornton's side to defend him from the violence generated by the strike. Their love is revealed in this sudden violent reaction to which both are vulnerable, and after many an error, their conjoined chemistry will overtake their political aversions. In their eventual attachment they provide the reconciliation between North and South, between capitalism and cooperation, that represents a similar solution to the great problems of industrialization offered by Charles Kingsley in *Alton Locke* and by Dickens in *Hard Times*. Professor Ingham regards this solution as spurious, and the attitude of Gaskell to her novel as intrinsically ambivalent.

This it might well be, if one regards it simply as a tractate on gender, class, or eroticism. But this is to ignore by far the magnificent moments as when Higgins (an alcoholic struggling to reform) refrains from intemperate speech in reaction to Thornton's hostile irritability. But neither does he back down or relinquish any of his dignity. Perhaps through Higgins Elizabeth Gaskell is administering a social lesson to John Stuart Mill (who thought no ideas of worth could come from the masses), when the working man responds to the owner's turned-friendly advice to keep his brains devoted to his own side of the divide. To which Higgins, speaking as an equal (or subject to subject) responds, "I shall need a deal o' brains to settle where my business ends and yo'rs begins" (319). How are the claims of labour and management to be adjudicated when it is so difficult to separate their several interests? Just as there are shifting sands between worker and management in their complex of issues and attitudes, so the same is true of North and South, where despite an active divide, there is still a needed reconciliation to the experience of change itself, which is Elizabeth Gaskell's great theme.

In *The Road to Wigan Pier* (chapter 7), George Orwell offers historical accounts for both the division between nations and also those that exist within nations. From Bodin and Botero we are familiar with the theorizing about Northern and Southern personality differences due to climate changes. Orwell disapprovingly summarizes their arguments. Given the driving force of nationalism, these influences worked their ways into standard history books for school children, there fostering and preserving a series of popular but spurious convictions. The Northerners are strong, energetic, and successful, while the Southerners are lazy, self-indulgent, and otherwise benighted. From this derives the English (Northern) prejudice against the Southerners. The inability of the Southerners to accept and adapt to the new methods and ways of the scientific, industrialized life of the North is given a biological basis, genetics opening the way to racism.

In *Geographies of England* (see pp. 5–6 above), in the essay quoted above in chapter 1, Ronald L. Martin addresses the cultural presentations of the North/South divide. The works of novelists and social commentators (he mentions ten of the most prominent) from the 1840s to the 1930s, are "rife" with "stereotypical" contrasts of the material conditions of life in the industrial and grimy North on the one hand and the idyllic South on the other. While not eager or willing to explore the statistical differences between the two areas, the presentations of these gifted writers are myths of personal consciousness, "passionate preferences," and ways of seeing the conditions of existence. That they are limited in what they see and are able to present in any work of art is not a handicap but rather a gift of insight. To cite one example, the last writer mentioned by Martin, D.H. Lawrence, as evidenced in his *Women in Love*, had already got wind of Taylorism, long before the statisticians could gauge its meaning and effects.[1]

When an Englishman headed north he seemed to be entering another country, with its miles upon miles of smoking chimneys, its simmering slag heaps. The industrialization of the North has given the North/South division a new and particular slant (Orwell 104). Following the language of Weber, and also the example of Thornton in Gaskell's *North and South*, Orwell describes the emergence of a "new type of man, the self-made Northern business man." When the two stories are told, the one of pre-industrialization and the other of the industrial age, with its mechanics and mechanisms of change, the issues being contested, the tone of action and its style will be quite different, but the continuities between the two historical divisions will remain.

By bringing the two epochs together, with their conducive, conceptual by-play, one of the major changes registered is that the North/South dichotomy can no longer sustain the vast extent and varieties of globalization. Yet, despite the elimination of that nominal geographic designation, the crucial fact remains that the countries that led the way to the pre-eminence of the North in the pre-industrial age, shall continue to be leaders in all facets of the new age, including science and technology, manufacturing industries and capitalism, colonialism, and trade. This fact makes it all the more necessary to begin the study of the great divide in the sixteenth century. A new and powerful engine has been added to the older one we have been tracking, one that draws the combined freights into the modern world.

This linkage, this development between the two epochs, only adds to the continuing strength and originating power of those Northern countries that gave us a wide spectrum of religious, political, and small every-day freedoms, Protestantism, a drastically new and productive sense of time, tolerance, and a healthy dose of scepticism, as well as their valuable by-products: commitment, the energies of faith and belief, and a hopefulness tempered by realism in the readiness to stride forward. In fact, Eric Hobsbawm, in *The Age of Revolution (1789–1848)*, the first instalment of his multi-volume study, writes of the consequences of the dual revolution (economic-industrial, and political – the French revolution) concluding with familiar language that this division between the advanced and "underdeveloped" countries proved to be "the most profound and most lasting" (181). The world he surveys is much larger than that of pre-industrialized Europe, in fact, it has become global. So he does not use the shorthand North/South denomination, but that is what his meaning includes. Contrasting the European "haves" with the rest of the world he excludes from the former "the Iberian peninsula" (although retaining Italy). Until the Soviet regime managed its great leap forward (perhaps overestimating the effectiveness of the second Soviet five-year plan), the chasm between the "backward" and the "advanced" continued to be "immoveable and untraversed" and was growing wider. Allowing for the difference of epochs and the difference of instruments under consideration, he utilizes the same thoughts and language, the aims as well as the argument of this book: "No fact has determined the history of the twentieth century more firmly than this" (181). In *The Age of Capital (1848–1875)*, Hobsbawm acknowledges that while "not in itself new," this dichotomy between the developed and underdeveloped countries, now on a much larger global scale, "begins to take on a recognizably modern shape" (305). This study of the early division of the North and the South substantiates the quoted phrase "not in itself new." Indeed, the close connection of the two epochs, and their prevailing spirits – the Great Divide begun in the sixteenth century and the "great Divergence" initiated in the era of industrialization – justifies the bold opening assertions of the Preface and of the first chapter: it offers a fundamental direction to the spreading appeal and value of what we have come to call the West.

Such an encomium representing the eulogistic part of the elegy could only set the stage for an obituary, and indeed, one must follow. The *force majeure* of the established world of bourgeois society and liberal values undergoes an inner collapse,[2] one of its very own making (*The Age of*

Empire 1875–1914). A philosophy gone barren combined with an inter-locking system of hostile alliances was sufficient to put an end to nearly a century of generalized peace. The great powers, the more advanced powers, i.e., the Northern powers became implicated in a tightly woven drama of mutual destruction. Described as "sleepwalkers" (more likely bewitched) they march to their own destruction – with a sense of hope-lessness and even greater disbelief. As with the story of Spain, multi-tudes of commentators explore the question of causation, needing to see what it was that cast such a spell upon them. Their assured mutual destruction is not visited upon them by a foreign power, rather it is endogenous, a crisis of intelligence and values at all levels of society. Yet, the summons of war, the "big" war that transforms error into vir-tue, restored a good portion of the sensible qualities that had once dis-tinguished the North – the sturdiness of conviction, the simplicity of affection and taste, and a resoluteness in pursuit of value.

There is no good way to bring this study to a close, because its issues are ever ongoing. Perhaps the simplest expedient is to end with these helpful works, all of them summary while directing ways forward. One chapter of the pre-industrial world closes here, but its very closure opens the ways to vastly expanded geographical boundaries and even more powerful individuals and explosive issues.

Shakespearean Silhouettes

It might seem strange to invoke Shakespeare here, but I sometimes find it easy to believe that in some of the issues treated in his plays and in even more of their characters, he has in mind the lurking shadows of Spain, its militaristic culture, its refusal to accept change and to live in the midst of ambiguity. Of course the subjects of the history plays are England and the English character, but they also cast shadows in which one can make out shapes of the Spanish character. Spain was after all the chief opponent, the threatening but defeated invader. And while English chronicles can produce drama enough, leverage is added when one senses a wider dramatic spell. Shakespeare had every reason to read into his English characters the features of Spanish characters: Spain had launched not one but several armadas against the English coast as a means of escorting the great general Farnese and his troops across the channel. So wary was the prudent Elizabeth of the Spanish powers that only very late did she consent to send money and contingents of troops to aid the Dutch in their rebellion against Philip II (she was not too fond of rebellion, even in Protestant causes). Spain and the Spanish character were very present to the English consciousness. For all the idiocies that attend the comparison of *Don Quixote* and Shakespeare's plays (spouted by the kind of people who dispute Shakespeare's authorship, declare Cervantes and Shakespeare to be the same person, and claim that Bacon had so much free time on his hands that he wrote both their works), there is a good reason why they may be brought together: the problems and characters of each were pan-European in their extent. This was the greatest of the sixteenth century discoveries, not so much the defeat of extravagant characters and wishes, but the recognition of something called reality, in which time is the primary agent. In this case time escapes its bounds and becomes a transcendent force in a metaphysical contest, a dramatic shift from the sacred to the secular. Its larger purpose is to provoke a diminishment in humankind's stature. "They told me I was everything," is Lear's great lament (anticipated by Richard II), only to add the anti-climax, "'Tis not true, I am not ague proof." The great age of the Renaissance witnessed such anti-climactic reductions. Encounters with or attempted escapes from reality are the common denominator of their works. Careless kings or vagrant knights were ruled by apparitions that had no basis in reality; in Vilar's phrase they were "unhinged from reality." Like Richard II they are heirs to eternity, soldiers of destiny, without any need to bend to the most sub-servient means of adjusting to the times. Their God, their faith is their protector. They can dispense with the time-world, with the necessary petty manoeuvres required. If we are to comprehend in terms of char-acter, and character immersed in philosophy, the diminished Spanish role, we must consult *Quixote*, but we should also make reference to Shakespeare. He and Cervantes are looking at the same experience but from different ends: Cervantes sees the full flowering of a world of illusions; Shakespeare recounts the awakening to this world, both in its tragic denouement (Richard and Hotspur) as well as in the timely realization of its fallaciousness. These are contemporary struggles of character, made for the stage, and of which, from his own English expe-rience, Shakespeare had an acute understanding. But going beyond his island to the continent of dreams provided his plays and their under-standing with added voltage and power. It is the map of Europe that he is addressing. Because Spain underwent quintessentially the trauma of the European character it suited well the drama of Shakespeare's plays. Only the Northern countries (including Shakespeare's England) were able to reject, to exorcise these burdensome types, these ghosts of emo-tional wilfulness that had no basis in reality. Thus in dramatizing these more extensive portraits of character – born out of his deep insight into the English themselves, their own urges to self-dramatization – Shake-speare was adding to the imaginative energy of his own plays, but was also giving us living portraits from Spain.

A sense of time is the leading agent in this new confrontation with reality. Time, then, mundane time, assumes colossal proportions throughout the Renaissance. It supports and verifies the greater theme of confrontation with reality, the reduction of the supposed grandeur of man to a creature hemmed in on all sides, burdened with guilt, ha-rassed by enemies, and showing small glimmers of future prospects.

Time in the Renaissance transcends itself. That one can dispense with the time-world is the dangerous fallacy from which tragic characters like Richard II or Milton's Satan never recover. The latter best summarizes the doomed belief in a world without consequence; he is

> One who brings
> A mind not to be changed by place or time.
> The mind is its own place, and in itself
> Can make a Heav'n of Hell, a Hell of Heav'n.   (I.252–5)

A kind of Gnostic sense of invulnerability, one that is beyond time and change, validates all actions and unites Shakespeare and Cervantes in their exposures of such empty boasting. Quixote's addled imagination certainly creates his own heaven out of hell. But the time-world of Shakespeare and of Milton means nothing if it does not mean a subjection to time, to historical circumstances, and to the edge of reality. Fictions cannot be validated by a sheer act of volition. As the ultra-realist Machiavelli instructed his readers, in order to control fortune or external events, one must first heed their prescriptions.

On a different level, in the choices presented to the Trojans in *Troilus and Cressida*, one can see transposed the character traits that prevented Spanish culture from adapting to the ways of change. In each one witnesses a failure to enter into the mental transactions of choice. In response to Paris and Troilus (*partis pris* if there ever were two) Hector advances every legitimate reason why the Trojans should return Helen to the Greeks and her rightful husband. But some blockage of will prevents him from acting on that principle. Finally and suddenly he reverts; there intercedes the fatal "nevertheless," that is, despite all the right reasons he can muster, that their "joint and several" dignities (honour) require their persistence in a war that has gone on far too long (II.v.163–93).

Notes

Preface

1 See Kenneth Pomeranz, *The Great Divergence: Europe, China and the Making of the Modern World Economy*.

1 Groundwork

1 In "A Reply to My Critics," *First Things*, June/July 2013:54.
2 Mme de Staël, I.V. 86, 90; 190–206. Certainly the most perceptive literary and social critic of her era, Mme de Staël writes lucidly of Voltaire and Rousseau, of the beginnings of Romanticism in Germany, and of literature in relation to social institutions; it is difficult, however, even to begin to understand her premise of human "perfectibility."
3 Geography and climate are two sources of confusion in any discussion of the causes of the great divisions in human societies.
4 Robert and Isabelle Tombs, *That Sweet Enemy: Britain and France. The History of a Love-Hate Relationship* (New York: Vintage, 2006).
5 The great Napoléon, prime reformer of many of the institutions of France (Corsica was purchased by France from Genoa one year before his birth in 1769), spoke with a decided southern accent.
6 There is one exception that comes to mind: "South, North, Nation ..." the title of Langton's essay in the collection *Geographies of England*. But in the body of that text they are always hyphenated, as North-South, with no exceptions.
7 Thomas Jefferson can be seen to participate in this racialistic adherence. Writing to a Major John Cartwright in June of 1824, he thanks him for sending a book on the English constitution and for having "deduced the Constitution of the English nation from its rightful root, the Anglo-Saxon"

(*Writings*, 1490). It was not until the expulsion of the "races of Plantagenets, Tudors and Stuarts" did the nation "re-enter into all its rights." In his *Autobiography* he justifies the amount of space dedicated to the unfolding of the French Revolution because he was living then in its midst, commenting on it with great sagacity, and noting its derivation from the American war of independence. The French are "the first of the European nations" to follow the American example. The next two sentences expand on this view: "From her the spirit (of rebellious defense of the rights of man) has spread over those of the South. The tyrants of the North have allied against it, but it is irresistible" (97). If the American revolution was considered as the headwater of the revolutionary movements of the early nineteenth century, particularly in the south of Europe, these uprisings were then construed as being against the overbearing powers of the North, viewed as regressive rather than economically and politically progressive.

8　This very useful phrasing comes from Albert O. Hirschman's *The Passions and the Interests* (Princeton: Princeton UP, 1977/1997).

9　Hirschman, 4–6.

10　Whether such "high points" become sore points, the "unintended" consequences of which had they been known would have been deplored, is a hypothetical which renders the point moot. Erasmus clearly saw into some of the adverse dimensions of Protestantism and regretted his participation in their defense and growth; Luther also clearly saw the coming time of war, but did not reject his assertive faith but rather felt it was an indication of God's revived presence in the world. Albert O. Hirschman invokes the principle of "unintended consequences" at the beginning of a movement but not later when sight becomes clearer and processes better defined. He exercises restraint in the fields examined, both in length of time and in limitation of subject. Perhaps only the duration of several hundred years provides an adequate canvas for a workable thesis, where one can see beginnings and ends, but to demand understanding and responsibility over a duration of more than four hundred years seems well beyond the pale. A book has recently appeared that in some instances runs parallel to *North/South*. Arguing for the continued vital presence of the factors of the Reformation and of the Enlightenment in the formation of the modern world is Brad S. Gregory's *The Unintended Reformation* (Harvard UP 2012). But the book veers off in a different direction, alleging that the living presence of the Reformation is an unfortunate, or unintended legacy, responsible for many of the errors and delusions of modern society, including among others, the ultimate "exclusion of God," "relativizing doctrines," "subjectivizing morality," and "secularizing knowledge." Coming together they sound like obscure diseases, or perhaps the flared inaccuracy of a blunderbuss.

At a distance of five hundred years, he detects behind all these deviations one major cause and infection: that is the reliance of mainline Protestants on "Scripture alone." This turned out to be no solution to the new problem, introduced by Protestantism, of how best to define the true nature of Christianity. Rather it compounded the problem by increasing the number of voices, all probing Holy Scripture for proof of their own positions. "This was the case throughout the Reformation era and has remained so ever since ... Hence the Reformation is the most important distant historical source of contemporary Western "hyperpluralism" with respect to truth claims about meaning, morality, values, priorities and purpose" (368–9). This is to write as if Babel and Pandemonium did not exist before and were uncontested after the Reformation.

Compactly stated this passage presents the overall argument, as well as the difficulties that are typical of this study, immensely learned as it is (with 145 pages of endnotes, compared with some 387 pages of text). Without foresight, this adherence to the doctrine of "Scripture alone," led to the proliferation of voluble sects with varying truth claims and the abiding modern problem of ... hyperpluralism, which is what? Which is something more numerous than pluralism, itself seeming to be acceptable whereas "hyper-" makes it less so. It would be interesting to know how much more abundant or numerous it is than pluralism. In short, where is the cut-off line? The value of Hirschman's arguments is that he tries to lay down some responsible ideas of duration, limits of responsibility, even of "unintended" consequences.

11 John Stuart Mill, *On Liberty*, eds. David Bromwich and George Kateb (New Haven: Yale UP, 2003).

12 Voltaire, *Romans et contes,* eds. Deloffre and van den Heuvel (Paris: Gallimard, 1979) 384–92. See also *Dictionnaire* (267) for a similar listing of the Northern tier of countries which "detached themselves" from the "Roman communion." But here the cause is "poverty," and the inability of the more impoverished North to support an opulent lifestyle and demands for more money from the Church. The North, in his words, assumed a new religion "at a better price" (*meilleur marché*), an inexcusable frivolity on Voltaire's part, perhaps offered only to meet the requirements of the alphabetized dictionary.

13 See Robert K. Massie, *Catherine the Great, Portrait of a woman* (New York: Random House, 2011) 172–3.

14 And were one to ask, "How does France rate in this catalogue of promising and progressive countries?" one would have to say, relying on the same *Princesse de Babylone,* not very well. In his discussion of the relevancy of Protestantism in the development of the northern tier, France does not

qualify by virtue of its subservience to the Roman papacy, which bestowed upon itself the doctrine of always being right (infallibility was then still a doctrine and not yet a dogma – 397). The portrayal of France is of a country divided between those who are idle, and spend their leisure time having fun and talking about the arts that others create, and those involved in religious disputes. While the idle party is somewhat feckless and silly, still they are harmless and serve to offset the hostilities of the fanatics. Voltaire follows this picture with recollections of the artistic grandeur of France from another time (that of the Great Century) and adds, as always, his own speculations as to why art forms and people rise and fall (398–400). One thought in particular is striking: Why, he asks, is the century where people have been taught to think clearly the one where they are brought to write so poorly? (n2, 1050). Is this the problem of the "liberal imagination?"

15 Mme de Staël credits the Protestant communities with doing away superstitious beliefs, with advancing virtuous conduct and with liberating philosophical speculation.

16 Trans. Talcott Parsons (New York: Scribner's, 1958). This remarkable volume will move in and out of this study, always provocative. However much open to criticism, there does seem to be some validity to the explanation in Weber's thesis of the connection between the prosperity and prominence of countries which experienced Reformation and the laggard countries which did not.

17 José Maravall, *Antiguos y modernos* (Madrid: Sociedad de Estudios, 1966).

2 Decline and Resistance

1 Carlo M. Cipolla, "The Economic Decline of Italy" in *The Economic Decline of Empires,* ed. Cipolla (London: Methuen, 1978).

2 This incidence of early Italian leadership only to be surpassed by Northern competition seems to be a pattern extending to other fields as well. According to Sven Beckert in his monumental *The Empire of Cotton* (2014) Italy owed its pre-eminence in cotton manufacturing to prior experience with wool and access to raw cotton (24). But it lost that leading position to "nimbler" German entrepreneurs because of its heavier restrictions: "high taxes, high wages, well-organized urban weavers and guild restrictions" (25). It suffered an even more damaging blow when the centre of trade shifted from the *entrepôts* of the Mediterranean to the Atlantic.

3 "Le Sac de Rome et la chute de Florence: l'asservissement de l'Italie" by Bonner Mitchell in *L'Époque de la Renaissance*, vol. iii, *Maturations et mutations* (1520–60) 35. *Rome* (New York: Knopf, 2011).

4 While an intrusion, this turn to Dostoevsky's Grand Inquisitor might be considered a welcome one. It shows the power of Dostoevsky's insight into Christian liberty and its developmental connection with latter-day French socialism. The fear wrought by this connection will send people scurrying back to the Church that has no room for the bad seed of Christian liberty – the newly reborn enemy of traditional sectarianism.

5 Quoted by Vives "The Economic Decline of Spain in the Seventeenth Century," in Cipolla, above chapter 1, n14.

6 Camus, "Ni victimes, ni bourreaux" 331, *Essais* (Paris: Gallimard, 1965).

7 Saint Augustine, *The City of God* (New York: Random House, 1950).

8 *Political Foundations of the Modern World*, vol. 2. *The Age of Reformation* (Cambridge: Cambridge UP, 1978). One of the strongest proponents of the belligerent role of religions is Mack P. Holt, *The French Wars of Religion*, 1562–1629 (Cambridge: Cambridge UP, 1995). But see also Karen Armstrong, *Fields of Blood, Religion and the History of Violence* (New York: Knopf, 2014).

3 The Challenge of Ideas

1 All references to Luther are to be found in the compact edition by John Dillenberger.

2 See the fundamental Book I.ix of the *Discourses* in *The Portable Machiavelli*, ed. and trans. Peter Bondanella and Mark Musa (New York: Penguin, 1979) 200–3. See also "Cain as Sacred Executioner" in Quinones, *The Changes of Cain* 62–83.

4 Tolerance Twin to Incredulity

1 Henry Kamen, *The Rise of Tolerance* (London: Weidenfeld and Nicolson, 1967) 13–15.

2 See *The Colloquies of Erasmus*, trans. Craig R. Thompson (Chicago: U Chicago P, 1965).

5 The Paradox of Time and the Moderns

1 William Butler Yeats, *The Collected Poems*.

2 *The Journal of the History of Ideas* 4 (1943): 51–6.

3 Also see David Landes (*The Wealth and Poverty of Nations* 174–8) for his arguments concerning Protestantism and time, both involved with his defense in theory and practice of Max Weber's notable thesis. In his earlier book, he remarks with surprise that Weber did not employ chronometric

arguments to support his thesis. In both books Landes makes the fundamental point that the exploitation of time was a decidedly Protestant awareness.

4 Article XLVI, "Idées Républicaines" in *Mélanges,* 327.

5 See Richard Ellmann's summation of Joyce's ethic in *James Joyce* (New York: Oxford UP, 1959) 756.

6 From "Little Gidding," *Four Quartets;* all citations of Eliot's poetry come from *The Complete Poems and Plays, 1909–1959* (New York: Harcourt and Brace, 1962).

7 See *The Renaissance Discovery of Time,* passim; and *Mapping Literary Modernism.*

8 See *Essays by Thomas Mann* (New York: Vintage, 1959) 173. Hobsbawm borrows the same phrasing in *The Age of Empire,* which "surveys the moment in history when it became clear that the society and civilization created by and for the western liberal bourgeoisie represented not the permanent form of the northern industrial world but only one phase of its early development" (11). Where Hobsbawm addresses bourgeois liberalism, Mann is considering liberal humanism – they are different sectors of the same issue; they both reclaimed that idea from Karl Marx.

9 Modernists are concerned with questions of being, not with making it, as is claimed for the nineteenth century novel, or having an inheritance reach the rightful person, or having an injustice corrected. These latter focuses concern the middling level, seeking some form of social justice or rightness. It is significant that in a modernist work no one is looking for a job or seeking their fortune, or inheritance; its aims are metaphysical, reaching beyond the social. Hence the presence of the epiphany, which opens another door to Modernist understanding. From Yeats's "The Magi" and "A Deep-sworn Vow" to "Easter 1916" there are apprehensions of levels of experience that go beyond the normal, the regular, the daily. "The Magi" may indeed have been the first of the Modernist efforts to inscribe the mythic method. The Modernist calling is both beneath and above the middle, the middle class, the middling way. It works in the midst of the collapse of humanism that Mann described.

6 Characters and Causality

1 "The Church in a Changing World," *Renaissance Studies* 166.

2 In *The Dutch Republic: Its Rise, Greatness and Fall, 1477–1806* 140. I have learned much from this masterwork, to which I am indebted for all future references to the events of this period that follow.

3 All quotations come from *The Apologie of Prince William of Orange Against the Proclamation of the King of Spain*; see also *The Apologie or Defense of the Most Noble Prince William*, Delft: 1581 (facs.); see also Israel n2 above, p. 210.

4 In Book V of his *République*, Bodin believes that the prince was exercising authority in the image of God. Bodin was a confirmed monarchist, who, like many others, supported a state solution to religious problems. Under the pressure of events he adopted the tolerant strategies of a *politique*.

5 From "North South," reprinted in chapter 7 of *The Road to Wigan Pier*, London: Secker and Warburg, 1937.

6 See the very useful *Dictionnaire de la pensée de Voltaire par lui-même*, ed. André Versaille.

7 See Roger Chartier, "The Saint-Malo – Geneva Line," from *Realms of Memory*, trans. Arthur Goldhammer, or from *Les lieux de Mémoire*, dir. Pierre Nora. Chartier resurrects from the work of Baron Dupin the line said to cut across France, separating the North from the South, by economic, natural, and intellectuals standards. From this line in the early nineteenth century the South became "underdeveloped" (471). To remedy this defect the South must begin to emulate the models of development, England and Scotland. The disparity between the "two Frances" may be remedied in this way. But other respondents citing differences in height, criminality, and pauperism – all to the disadvantage of the North – argue that industrialization is not all it is cracked up to be (477). But as always happens, divisions yield themselves to further subdivisions, until the North-South divide is dissipated into various and vying regions and methodologies. Chartier's conclusions restore the North-South polarity, but also find that the "gap" between the two sectors "alone" no longer "seems sufficient to account for certain long-term disparities and imbalances" (496). In Alain Corbin's masterful essay, "Divisions of Time and Space," ibid. where *la province* is like a discarded highway alongside the new *autoroute* that is Paris, he follows the wandering courses of *la province* in relation to the burgeoning city, concluding that "France, south of the Loire, especially the Midi, is like exacerbated provinces" (429). A valuable introductory course in French literature and culture could be construed from this history of the Paris-*province* dualism.

8 Entering into this concern with causality is Jared Diamond's *Guns, Germs and Steel*. The authors in this book are concerned with culture and civilization, what Diamond would call "proximate" causes, while his interests measure the effects of thousands of years and what he considers "deeper" or more ultimate causes. He moves the argument from climatology to vast

stretches of geographic time. What are the bases for certain areas taking hold and not others, for their growth and survival?

The conclusion of the chapter "The Collision at Cajamarca" can serve as a fulcrum that establishes the triumph of proximate causes and looks beyond to the need for "ultimate" causes. When Pizarro's small legions of Spaniards subdued Atahuallpa and his far more numerous forces of thousands of Incas, that was a victory born out of the book's title. But here not even their guns were of much avail, cumbersome as they were and slow to load and reload. But steel plated armor, helmets, swords, and lances were strength enough to protect the Spanish forces and defeat the Incas. The availability of such advanced technology, in addition to the powers of the horse and the art of letters, resulted in the Europeans colonizing the New World, rather than the reverse. But this explanation resorts to "proximate" causes and does not address the "fundamental" question as to why these advantages should have accrued to the European states when they did not to the many native states of the world. To ask these questions is to ask "deeper" questions of "ultimate causation" (80–1).

Succeeding readable pages then discuss in technical but not over-bearing language the ways that over a period of 10,000 to 13,000 years certain intercontinental areas were able to domesticate plants and animals. This transformed their lives and eventually provided the means for technological growth. "Sedentary living was essential, decisive for the history of technology" (261). The next step was the spread and diffusion of the acquired skills to neighbouring bodies, either by imitation or by "engulfing." Thus centres of industry and advancement developed. The Eurasian axis along a limited latitudinal range was particularly fruitful as there were few natural blocks to passage. Europe and China emerged as engines of change. But then the question arises – similar to the one coming from the European conquest of Peru – as to How China Became China (chapter 16).

My argument with this study it is not with its wealth of information and examples but rather with its claims. By providing geographical explanations of how continents are developed and considering these tens of thousands of years as "ultimate" causes, might not Diamond invite comparisons with astrophysics dealing with the much longer time schemes of galaxies? The extent of years and whether or not causes are "proximate" might well be considered relative to magnifications of distances. According to these calculations even geographical causes may be reduced to being "proximate." Furthermore, to regard the changes Diamond records as being "deeper" than "proximate" causes of culture and civilization is to confuse extensiveness with intensiveness, background with foreground.

They may set the stage but they are not the drama. They are necessary but not sufficient. They provide the rock and the hill, but Sisyphus must push the rock up the hill. Or, to borrow from Camus's dualistic rival, Sartre, the physical mountain might be present, but it depends upon human agent's freedom to climb the mountain. Proximate causes are not subordinate but cover large enough periods of time; even five hundred years seem quite sufficient for many of us.

7 Centring the Great Bases in Thought

1 See p. 16 above, William James.
2 The ever-lively responsiveness of Heiko Oberman in *Luther: Between God and Devil*, lends some support to the differences sketched in here. For him Luther's marriage counsel "bursts the seams of moral convention," adding "biblical counsel is not to be confused with bourgeois morality." Such a "human all too human" response is "different from the Reformation in the cities and from Calvin's Reformation" (288–9). Like Oberman, Lewis Spitz regards Luther and Calvin as representing two surges of the Reformation advance, whatever their differences. The Calvinist, convinced of election [he was among the "chosen"] and assured of preservation in faith, developed a heroic activism in the world … [he] was noted for self-discipline, rigid morality, an inclination toward legalism, and a strong sense of vocation not only to the religious life but to secular occupation as well. The Calvinists developed a certain moral earnestness and a militancy not found among the evangelical Christians" (*The Protestant Reformation* 1517–59). And naturally, there arises before us the image of the future economic man of capitalist and industrial expansion.

8 English Thought: John Milton, John Locke, and John Stuart Mill

1 A fellow exile with Locke in the United Provinces was another *contre-révocationnaire*, Pierre Bayle. Together while apart – they did know one another – they demonstrate the big push given to tolerance by the Revocation of the Edict of Nantes. In fact, they share many of the propositions in favor of tolerance, one of them being a very broad English latitudinarianism. The great stumbling block for both of them, as for William I, to an unlimited practice of toleration, were Catholics and their allegiance to Rome. See O'Cathasaigh, "Bayle and Locke on Tolerance, " in *De l'Humanisme aux Lumières, Bayle et le protestantisme*, eds. M. Magdelaine et al., 687–9. But despite their similarities and their presence as fellow refugees in the United

provinces, Locke and Bayle were radically different. Bayle is the most complicated mind of his generation. He defends an absolute monarchy, and is a convinced realist. He shares little of his fellow exiles' messianic dreams of a grand return to France under the gilded wings of William III. He is tired of the long and bitter exchange of hostilities between the refugees. Their place of refuge is an intellectual cockpit where their isolation seems to produce two qualities: caricature of enemies and dangerous republicanism. Intellectually Bayle seems to be a fideist, another of the gifted children of Montaigne. His attitudes are a composite of scepticism and tolerance. His religious ideas went against the common-places of his time. All the aspects of his personality, his place among the refugees, and his intellectual distance inclined him toward his last and greatest work, the *Dictionnaire critique,* where he, as a hunter, was determined to chase down the errors of the previous compilations. See Hubert Bost's splendid biography, *Bayle.*

2 *On Liberty*, eds. Bromwich and Kateb, 28.

3 Marx, in the *Manifesto of the Communist Party*, means by this phrase "the class of modern capitalists, owners of the means of social production and employers of wage-labor."

4 To regard him as the last requires an elucidation of the corollary term "the first." They are both terms of consequence, the one yielding continuity and the other termination. As there are "firsts," so there are "lasts," each elusive, the one receding into the past, covered by the "dark backward and abysm of time"; the other surpassed by contingencies, the unknown products of an impalpable future. Each reveals the attenuation of chronological determinations (see 112 above). There is one notable test case that provides some standards for judgment and that is the laureatization of Petrarch. On 8 April 1341 Petrarch was crowned with the laurel on the Campidoglio in Rome, thus reviving the ancient practice that had fallen into disuse. Statius may have been the last to be so crowned. But there is some question to the claim that Petrarch was the first in the reborn custom. Albertino Mussato had been so crowned in Padua in 1315, and Dante in the most beautiful prelude to *Paradiso* XXV determines not to accept the *ghirlanda* (Boccaccio seems to intimate that one was on the way to being offered before Dante's sudden death) except in the place where he entered the Christian faith by way of baptism. There – in the Baptistery of Florence – at the right beginning of his life would he have crowned the right ending.

In short, there were consequences to Petrarch's recognition, a trail of consequence amidst followers. The companion document, the letter to King Robert of Sicily (*Fam.* IV. 7) explains the twofold nature of Renaissance creative humanism. Petrarch addresses the classical situation of the aspiring writer. The writers of the past, dead and gone, are held up as paragons in comparison with whom contemporary efforts are demoted. He cites examples from Roman culture in which some critics declared the great age to be over – this right before the advent of Virgil, Horace, and Ovid. Far from giving up Petrarch urges his contemporaries to aspire to greatness: let us try, let us endeavour. *Enitamur, speremur*. He quotes Virgil: if we try we shall succeed. And so it happened. When Cassirer speaks of the dynamic of the Renaissance it is this great and confident faith in hopeful effort that is meant. Petrarch's oration urging high endeavour was the confirmation, the royal seal was the coronation. The laureatization of Petrarch may be considered the first because of these two practices: a signal event, the actual crowning, and the attendant pronouncement of a poetics that thrived during the following centuries. Like Mill's "last," it does not only hold to the present but reaches far into the past, and helps determine or acknowledge the substance of the unknown future.

9 The Edict of Nantes, Toleration, and Voltaire

1 But as John D. Woodbridge maintains it was more by disregard that under Louis XV (1755) some of the Huguenots would "no longer be willing to assemble in clandestine meetings for their worship services; now they were attempting to worship in fixed buildings"; "An eighteenth century fronde?" *De l'Humanisme aux Lumières*, ed. Michelle Magdalaine et al., 79–93.
2 One can stake such a claim for Louis XIV without being blind to his defects, which, however, are probably not absent in any other monarch of this and later epochs.

10 The Pending Revival of the South

1 New York: Random House Vintage, 1979. A brief quotation from p. 3 can give the tone of this much-praised and important volume: "In short, Orientalism is a Western style for dominating, restructuring and having authority over the Orient." It has some relevancy for "meridionalism."
2 In a chapter entitled, "The Return of the Global South," Sven Beckert describes the various ways that "the world's cotton industry returned to where it had largely originated," that is, to China and India (382). And formerly far-and-away leaders in the booming cotton industry, Liverpool and Manchester, and the Fall River area of Massachusetts, were victimized by the "rush to the bottom," that is, Northern industrial suppliers – and this is

pan-Northern – pulling up stakes and following the paths of ever cheaper labor, undisturbed by matters such as unions and the franchise.

3 In his "Grand Tour" Mead adds some piquant reactions from Voltaire, who claims Spain was as little known as the deepest parts of Africa and that it was not worth the trouble of being known (252). Thus, the anti-Enlightenment measures of Spain receive their rewards.

4 One should also mention the promising publishing series *Les Écritures du Sud* in which the excellent study of Lafont first appeared.

5 Thomas Mermall, ed. Ortega y Gasset, José, *La rebelión de las masas.*

6 See the essays adjoined to *The Theme of Our Time*, wherein he discusses: the idea that perspective is one of the component parts of reality (90); the demotion of high seriousness, to be compared with Eliot's promotion of "wit"; the theory of Einstein in its historical significance, one aspect of which is the respect shown to other cultures. The list of his contributions is copious.

7 Rogers, 88 ff.

8 For Elliott, see pp. 24–5 above.

9 Simone Weil, "Attention et la volonté," *La pesanteur et la grâce* 192.

11 Towards a Summation

1 See Quinones, *Mapping Literary Modernism* 76, 81.

2 See Christopher Clark, *The Sleepwalkers, How Europe Went to War in 1914* (New York: HarperCollins, 2013).

Works Cited and Consulted

Ahnlund, Nils. *Gustav Adolph the Great*. Trans. Michael Roberts. Princeton: Princeton UP, 1940. Print.

Armstrong, Karen. *Fields of Blood: Religion and the History of Violence*. New York: Knopf, 2014. Print.

Aston, Trevor, ed. *Crisis in Europe 1560–1660*. Garden City, NY: Doubleday Anchor, 1967. Print.

Augustine. *The City of God*. New York: Random, 1950. Print.

Augustijn, Cornelius. *Erasmus: Der Humanist als Theologe und Kirchenreformer*. Leiden: Brill, 1996. Print.

– *Erasmus: His Life, Work, and Influence*. Trans. J.C. Grayson. Toronto: U of Toronto P, 1991. Print.

Bainton, Roland. *Erasmus of Christendom*. New York: Scribner's, 1969. Print.

Baker, Alan R.H., and Mark Billinge. *Geographies of England: The North-South Divide, Imagined and Material*. Cambridge: Cambridge UP, 2004. Print.

Baldini, Enzo A., ed. *Botero e la "Ragione di Stato."* Florence: Olschki, 1992. Print.

Bataillon, Marcel. "Actualité d'Érasme." *Colloquia Erasmiana Turonensia*. Tours, 1969. 1871–90. Print.

– *Érasme et L'Espagne*. Paris: Droz, 1937. Print.

Bayle, Pierre. "Avis important aux réfugiés." *Les Fondements philosophiques de la Tolérance*. Ed. Y.C. Zarka et al. Vol. 2. Paris: PUF, 2004. 333–59. Print.

Bessire, François, and Sylvain Menant, eds. *Traité sur la tolérance de Voltaire*. Paris: Édition du Temps, 1999. Print.

Besterman, Theodore. *Voltaire*. 3rd ed. Chicago: U of Chicago P, 1976. Print.

– gen. ed. *Studies on Voltaire and the Eighteenth Century*. Vols. 145–7. Oxford: The Voltaire Foundation, 1976. Print.

Billinge, Mark, and Alan R.H. Baker, eds. *Geographies of England: The North-South Divide, Material and Imagined*. Cambridge: Cambridge UP, 2004. Print.

Blumenberg, Hans. *The Legitimacy of the Modern Age*. Trans. Robert M. Wallace. Cambridge: MIT, 1983. Print.

Boccaccio, Giovanni. The *Decameron*. Trans. Mark Musa and Peter Bondanella. New York: Mentor, 1982. Print.

Bodin, Jean. *Six Books of the Commonwealth*. Trans. M.J. Tooley. Oxford: Basil Blackwell, 1955. Print.

– *La Méthode de l'histoire*. Trans. P. Mesnard. Paris: Société d'Édition, 1941. Print.

– *Les six livres de la république (Livre cinquième)*. Vol. 5. Paris: Fayard, 1986. Print.

Bornkamm, Heinrich. "Erasmus und Luther." *Das Jahrhundert der Reformation*. 2nd ed. Gottingen: Vandenhoeck and Ruprecht, 1966. Print.

– *Luther in Mid-Career, 1521–1530*. Trans. E. Theodore Bachmann. Philadelphia: Fortress, 1983. Print.

Bost, Hubert. *Bayle*. Paris: Fayard, 2006. Print.

Botero, Giovanni. *The Reason of State*. Trans. P.J. and D.P. Waley. London: Routledge & Kegan Paul, 1956. Print.

Bouretz, Pierre. *Les Promesses du Monde*. Paris: Gallimard, 1996. Print.

Bouwsma, William J. *The Waning of the Renaissance 1550–1640*. New Haven: Yale UP, 2000. Print.

Brann, Eva. *Homage to Americans*. Philadelphia: Paul Dry, 2010. Print.

Brecht, Martin. *Martin Luther. Shaping and Defining the Reformation 1521–1532*. Vol. 2. Trans. James L. Schaaf. Minneapolis: Fortress, 1994. Print.

Brzezinski, Zbigniew. *Strategic Vision, America and the Crisis of Global Power*. New York: Basic, 2012. Print.

Butler, Clark. *The Dialectical Method*. New York: Humanity, 2012. Print.

Camus, Albert. *Essais*. Paris: Gallimard, 1965. Print.

Carr, Raymond, ed. *Spain: A history*. New York: Oxford UP, 2000. Print.

Cassano, Franco. *Southern Thought and Other Essays on the Mediterranean*. Ed. and trans. Norma Bouchard and Valerio Ferme. New York: Fordham University Press, 2012. Print.

Cassirer, Ernst. *The Philosophy of the Enlightenment*. 1932. Trans. F.C.A. Koelln and J.P. Pettegrove. Boston: Basic, 1955. Print.

– *The Question of Jean-Jacques Rousseau*. Trans. Peter Gay. New York: Columbia UP, 1954. Print.

– "Remarks on the Originality of the Renaissance," *Journal of the History of Ideas* 4 (1943). 51–6. Print.

Cervantes Saavedra, Miguel de. *Don Quixote*. Trans. Edith Grossman. New York: Harper Collins, 2003. Print.

Chartier, Roger. *Les lieux de Mémoire*. Gen. ed. Pierre Nora. 7 vols. Paris: Gallimard, 1993. Print.

– "The Saint-Malo – Geneva Line." *Realms of Memory*. Vol. 1. Trans. Arthur Goldhammer. New York: Columbia UP, 1996. 467–96. Print.

Cioran, E.M. *La chute dans le temps*. Paris: Gallimard, 1964. Print.

Cipolla, Carlo M., ed. *The Economic Decline of Empires*. London: Methuen, 1970. Print.

– "The Economic Decline of Italy." *The Economic Decline of Empires*. Ed. Cipolla. 196–214. Print.

Clark, Christopher. *The Sleepwalkers: How Europe Went to War in 1914*. New York: Harper, 2013. Print.

Coleridge, Samuel Taylor. *The Collected Works of Samuel Taylor Coleridge, The Friend II*. Ed. Barbara E. Rooke. London: Routledge & Kegan Paul, 1969. Print.

Cronk, Nicholas, ed. *The Cambridge Companion to Voltaire*. Cambridge: Cambridge UP, 2009. Print.

Dainotto, Roberto M. *Europe (In Theory)*. Durham and London: Duke UP, 2007. Print.

Davis, Kathleen. *Periodization and Sovereignty*. Philadelphia: University of Pennsylvania Press, 2008. Print.

Delumeau, Jean, ed. *L'acceptation de l'autre (de l'Èdit de Nantes à nos jours)*. Paris: Fayard, 2000. Print.

Deyon, Solange. "Les édits avant l'Édit." *L'Édit de Nantes (1598), La France et l'Europe*. Ed. Joblin. Print.

Diamond, Jared. *Guns, Germs and Steel*. New York: Norton, 2005. Print.

Dickens, Charles. *Hard Times for These Times*. 1854. London: Penguin Classics, 1993. Print.

Dillenberger, John. *Martin Luther, Selections from His Writings*. New York: Anchor, 1962. Print.

Dolan, John. *The Essential Erasmus*. New York: Meridian, 1983. Print.

Dostoevsky, Fyodor. *The Brothers Karamazov*. Ed. with revised trans. Ralph Matlaw. New York: Norton Critical Edition, 1976. Print.

Edict of Nantes (1598–1998). *L'Édit de Nantes: texte intégrale en français moderne*. Ed. Danièle Thomas et al. Bizanos: Héraclès, 1998. Print.

Eliot, T.S. *The Complete Poems and Plays, 1909–1959*. New York: Harcourt and Brace, 1962. Print.

Elliott, J.H. "The Decline of Spain." *Europe in Crisis 1560–1660*. Ed. Aston. 176–93. Print.

– *Europe Divided, 1559–1598*. New York: Harper Torchbook, 1968. Print.

– *Imperial Spain*. New York: St Martin's, 1965. Print.

Ellmann, Richard. *James Joyce*. New York: Oxford, 1959. Print.

Erasmus, Desiderius. "The Education of a Christian Prince." *Collected Works of Erasmus*. Vol. 27. Toronto: U Toronto P: 1986. Print.

– *On Mending [Restoring] the Peace of the Church* (*De sarcienda ecclesiae concordia* 1533). Trans. John P. Dolan. *The Essential Erasmus.* New York: Meridian, 1983. 331–83. Print.

– *The Polemics of Erasmus of Rotterdam and Ulrich von Hutten.* Trans. Randolph J. Klawiter. Notre Dame: U Notre Dame P, 1977. Print.

– *Querela Pacis.* Ed. O. Herding. *Erasmi Opera Omnia IV-2.* Amsterdam: North Holland, 1977. Print.

Ferguson, Wallace K. *Europe in Transition 1300–1520.* Boston: Houghton, 1962. Print.

– *Renaissance Studies.* New York: Harper, 1963. Print.

– "The Attitude of Erasmus toward Toleration." *Renaissance Studies.* 75–83. Print.

– "The Church in the Changing World: A Contribution to the Interpretation of the Renaissance." *Renaissance Studies.* 155–70. Print.

– "The Reinterpretation of the Renaissance; Suggestion for a Synthesis." *Renaissance Studies.* 125–36. Print.

– "Toward the Modern State." *Renaissance Studies.* 137–53. Print.

Feros, Antonio, and Juan Gelabert, eds. *España en Tiempos del Quijote.* Madrid: Taurus Historia, 2004. Print.

Fernández-Armesto, Felipe. "The Improbable Empire." *Spain: A History.* Ed. Carr. 116–50. Print.

Fernández-Armesto, Felipe and Derek Wilson. *Reformations: A Radical Interpretation of Christianity and the World, 1500–2000.* New York: Scribner's, 1996. Print.

Frost, Robert. *The Poetry of Robert Frost.* New York: Holt, Rinehart and Winston, 1975. Print.

Findlay. J.N. *Hegel: A Re-examination.* New York: Macmillan, 1958. Print.

Garrisson, Janine. "L'Édit de Nantes." *Édit de Nantes revisité.* Ed. Hubler et al. 9–14. Print.

Gaskell, Elizabeth. *North and South (1855).* London: Penguin Classics, 2003. Print.

Gelabert, Juan, and Antonio Feros, eds. *España en Tiempos del Quijote.* Madrid: Taurus Historia, 2004. Print.

Gibbon, Edward. *The Decline and Fall of the Roman Empire.* 2 vols. New York: The Modern Library, 1932. Print.

Gopnik, Adam. "Faces, Places, Spaces." *The New Yorker* 29 Oct. 2012. Print.

Grady, Hugh. *The Modernist Shakespeare.* Oxford: Clarendon, 1991. Print.

Gregory, Brad. S. *The Unintended Reformation: How a Religious Revolution Secularized Society.* Cambridge, MA: Harvard UP, 2012. Print.

Hamilton, Earl J. *American Treasure and the Price Revolution in Spain, 1501–1650.* Cambridge, MA: Harvard UP, 1934. Print.

Hart, Jonathan. *Comparing Empires.* New York: Palgrave Macmillan, 2003. Print.

Haile, H.G. *Luther.* Garden City, NY: Doubleday, 1980. Print.

Haskins, Charles Homer. *The Renaissance of the Twelfth Century.* 1927. New York: Meridian, 1955. Print.

Healy, Thomas. *The Great Dissent.* New York: Henry Holt, 2013. Print.

Hegel, Georg W.F. *The Philosophy of History.* Trans. J. Sibree. New York: Prometheus, 1991. Print.

– *Die Vernunft in der Geschichte.* Ed. Johannes Hoffmeister. Berlin: Akademie, 1970. Print.

– *Die Philosophie der Geschichte.* Ed. Klaus Vieweg. Jena: Fink, 2005. Print.

– *Hegel Selections.* Ed. M.J. Inwood. New York: Macmillan, 1989. Print.

– *Reason in History: A General Introduction.* Ed. Robert S. Hartman. New York: Bobbs Merrill, 1953. Print.

– Hegel: *Lectures on the Philosophy of Religion.* Ed. Peter G. Hogdson. Berkeley: U California P, 1988. Print.

– Hegel, *The Essential Writings.* Ed. Frederick G. Weiss. New York: Harper & Row, 1974. Print.

– *La Raison dans l'histoire.* Trans. K. Papaioannou. Paris: Plon, 1965. Print.

Heidegger, Martin. *Basic Writings.* Revised and expanded edition. San Francisco: Harper Collins, 1997. Print.

– *Being and Time.* Trans. Joan Stambaugh. New York: SUNY, 1996. Print.

Heuvel, Jacques van den. *Voltaire dans ses contes.* Paris: Armand Colin, 1967. Print.

Hillerbrand, Hans J., ed. *Erasmus and His Age: Selected Letters of Desiderius Erasmus.* New York: Harper Torch, 1970. Print.

Hirschman, Albert O. *The Passions and the Interests: Political Arguments for Capitalism before Its Triumph.* Princeton: Princeton UP, 1977/1997. Print.

Hobsbawm, E.J. *The Age of Capital (1848–1875).* New York: Random House Vintage, 1996. Print.

– *The Age of Empire (1875–1914).* New York: Random House Vintage, 1989. Print.

– *The Age of Extremes (1914–1991) New York*: Pantheon, 1994. Print.

– *The Age of Revolution (1789–1848).* New York: Random House Vintage, 1996. Print.

– "The Crisis of the Seventeenth Century." *Crisis in Europe 1560–1660.* Ed. Aston. 5–58. Print.

Höffding, Harrald. *A History of Modern Philosophy,* vol 2. New York: Dover, 1955. Print.

Holt, Mack P. *The French Wars of Religion, 1562–1629.* Cambridge: Cambridge UP, 1955. Print.

Hubler, Lucienne, et al., eds. *L'Édit de Nantes Revisité*. Geneva: Droz, 2000. Print.

Huizinga, Johan. *Erasmus and the Age of Reformation*. New York: Harper & Row, 1957. Print.

Iarocci, Michael. *Properties of Modernity*. Nashville: Vanderbilt UP, 2006. Print.

Ingham, Patricia. Introduction. *North and South*. By Elizabeth Gaskell. London: Penguin Classics, 2003. Print.

Israel, Jonathan I. *Radical Enlightenment: Philosophy and the making of modernity*. Oxford: Oxford UP, 2001. Print.

– "Enlightenment? Which Enlightenment?" *Journal of the History of Ideas* 67 (2006). Print.

– *The Dutch Republic: Its Rise, Greatness, and Fall: 1477–1806*. Oxford: Clarendon, 1995. Print.

James, William. *The Varieties of Religious Experience*. New York: Modern Library, 1936. Print.

Joblin, Alain, ed. *L'Édit de Nantes (1598), la France et l'Europe*. Arras: Artois PU, 1998. Print.

Joyce, James. *Finnegans Wake*. New York: Viking, corrected 1955. Print.

Kamen, Henry. *The Spanish Inquisition*. London: Weidenfeld and Nicolson, 1965. Print.

– *The Rise of Tolerance*. London: Weidenfeld and Nicolson, 1967. Print.

Kagan, Robert. *The World America Made*. New York: Alfred A. Knopf, 2012. Print.

Kingsley, Charles. *Alton Locke*. New York: Dolphin, 1961. Print.

Klawiter, Randolph J. *The Polemics of Erasmus and Ulrich von Hutten*. Notre Dame: U Notre Dame P, 1977. Print.

Kushner, Eva. *Maturations et mutations (1520–1560)*. Vol. 3 of *L'Époque de la Renaissance*. Philadelphia: Benjamins, 2011. Print.

Lafont, Robert. *Le Sud ou L'autre: La France et son Midi*. Aix-en-Provence: Sari Édisud, 2004. Print.

Landes, David. *The Wealth and Poverty of Nations*. New York: W.W. Norton, 1998. Print.

– *Revolution in Time*. Cambridge, MA: Harvard UP, 1983. Print.

Langton, John. "South, North and Nation," *Geographies of England*. Eds. Baker and Billinge. 112–44. Print.

Lawrence, D.H. *Women in Love*. New York: Viking Compass, 1960. Print.

Le Roy Ladurie, Emmanuel. "Nord/Sud," *Les Lieux de Mémoire*, gen. ed. Pierre Nora. Paris: Gallimard, 1993. Print.

Lestringant, Frank. "La résistance Huguenote à l'édit de Nantes; le cas d'Agrippa d'Aubigné." *L'Édit de Nantes Revisité*. Ed. Hubler et al. 20–40. Print.

Levin, Harry. *The Implications of Literary Criticism*. Ed. Jonathan Hart. Paris: Honoré Champion, 2011. Print.

- *Playboys and Killjoys*. New York: Oxford University Press, 1987. Print.

Levine, Alan, ed. *Early Modern Skepticism and the Origins of Toleration*. New York: Lexington, 1999. Print.

Lewis, Bernard. *The End of Modern History in the Middle East*. Stanford: Hoover Institution Press, 2011. Print.

- *The Crisis of Islam*. New York: Random House, 2004. Print.

Locke, John. *A Letter Concerning Toleration (In Focus)*. New York: Routledge, 1991. Print.

- *Locke on Toleration*. Cambridge: CUP, 2010. Print.

- *The Reasonableness of Christianity*. Stanford: Stanford UP, 1958. Print.

Luther, Martin. *Selections from His Writings*. Ed. John Dillenberger. New York: Anchor, 1962. Print.

Machiavelli, Niccolò. *Discorsi. Tutte le opere*. Eds. Francesco Flora and Carlo Cordie. Florence: Mondadori, 1968. Print.

Magdelaine, M., et al., eds. *De l'Humanisme aux Lumières, Bayle et le protestant-isme*. Oxford: Voltaire Foundation, 1999. 687–9. Print.

Mann, Thomas. *Essays*. Trans. H.T. Lowe-Porter. New York: Vintage, 1957. Print.

Maravall, José. *Antiguos y modernos*. Madrid: Sociedad de Estudios, 1966. Print.

Martin, Ronald L. "The Contemporary Debate over the North-South Divide." *Geographies of England*. Eds. Baker and Billlinge. 15–43. Print.

Marx, Karl. "*Manifesto of the Communist Party.*" *Selected Works of Karl Marx and Frederick Engels*. New York: International Publishers, 1974. 35–63. Print.

Mattingly, Garrett. *The Armada*. New York: Houghton-Mifflin, 1959. Print.

Mead, William Edward. *The Grand Tour in the Eighteenth Century*. 1914. New York: Benjamin Bloom, 1972. Print.

Menchi, Silvana Seidel. *Erasmo in Italia, 1520–1580*. Torino: Bollati Boringhieri, 1987. Print.

Mermall, Thomas, ed. Ortega y Gasset, José. *La rebelión de las masas*. Madrid: Castali, 1998. Print.

Mervaud, Christiane. "Tolérance religieuse et pouvoir politique dans le *Traité sur la tolérance*." *Traité sur la tolérance de Voltaire*. Eds. Bessire et Menant. 51–70. Print.

Mill, John Stuart. *Essays on Politics and Society*. Vols. XVIII–XIX. Toronto and Buffalo: U of Toronto Press, 1977. Print.

- *On Liberty*. Ed. David Bromwich and George Kateb. New Haven: Yale University Press, 2003. Print.

- *The Basic Writings of John Stuart Mill*. Ed. Dale E. Miller. New York: Harper Torchbook, 2002. Print.

Milton, John. *The Prose of John Milton*. Ed. J. Max Patrick. New York: Anchor, 1967. Print.

Mitchell, Bonner. "Le Sac de Rome et la chute de Florence: l'asservissement de l'Italie." *Maturations et Mutations (1520–1660)*. Ed. Kushner. 35–42. Print.

Mout, M.E.H.N, et al., eds. *Erasmianism: Idea and Reality*. Amsterdam: 1997. Print.

Montesquieu, Baron. *De l'Esprit des Lois*, vol. 2. Ed. Robert Derathé. Paris: Classiques Garnier, 1973. Print.

Naves, Raymond. *Voltaire*. 8th ed. Paris: Hatier, 1972. Print.

Nuttall, A.D. *Shakespeare the Thinker*. New Haven: Yale UP, 2007. Print.

Oberman, Heiko O. *Luther: Man between God and the Devil*. Trans. Eileen Walliser-Schwartzbart. New York: Doubleday, 1992. Print.

Ogg, David. *Europe in the 17th Century*, 6th ed. London: Adam and Charles Black, 1952. Print.

O'Rourke Boyle, Marjorie. "The Eponymns of Desiderius Erasmus." *Renaissance Quarterly* 30.1 (Spring 1977):12–23. Print.

Ortega y Gasset, José. *La rebelión de las masas*. Ed. Thomas Mermall. Madrid: Castali, 1998. Print.

– *The Modern Theme*. New York: Harper Torchbooks, 1961. Print.

Orwell, George. *The Road to Wigan Pier*. London: Secker & Warburg, 1959. Print.

Peretó Rivas, Rubén. *Tolerancia: Teoría y Práctica en la Edad Media*. Porto: Fédération Internationale des Instituts d'Études Médiévales, 2012. Print.

Pomeau, René. *Ecraser l'Infâme*. Oxford: Voltaire Foundation, 1994. Print.

– "L'affaire Calas." *Traité sur la tolérance de Voltaire*. Eds. Bessire et Menant. 25–31. Print.

– *D'Arouet à Voltaire*. Oxford: Voltaire Foundation, 1985. Print.

– *De la Cour au jardin*. Oxford: Voltaire Foundation, 1991. Print.

– *On a voulu l'enterrer*. Oxford: Voltaire Foundation, 1994. Print.

Pomeranz, Kenneth. *The Great Divergence: Europe, China and the Making of the Modern World Economy*. New York: Macmillan Palgrave, 2000. Print.

Quinones, Ricardo J. *Dualisms: The Agons of the Modern World*. Toronto: U of Toronto P, 2007. Print.

– *Erasmus and Voltaire: Why They Still Matter*. Toronto: U of Toronto P, 2010. Print.

– *Mapping Literary Modernism*. Princeton: Princeton UP, 1985. Print.

– *The Changes of Cain*. Princeton: Princeton UP, 1991. Print.

– *The Renaissance Discovery of Time*. Cambridge: Harvard UP, 1972. Print.

Rabelais, Francois. *Gargantua. Oeuvres complètes*. Ed. Pierre Jourda. Paris: Garnier, 1962. Print.

Riesman, David, et al. *The Lonely Crowd*. New Haven: Yale UP. 1950. Print.

Roberts, Michael. *Gustavus Adolphus: 1626–1632*. Vol. 2 of *Gustavus Adolphus: A History of Sweden 1611–1632*. London: Longmans, Green, 1958. Print.

Rogers, Gayle. *Modernism and the New Spain*. New York: Oxford UP, 2012. Print.

Rousseau, André Michel. Preface. *Studies on Voltaire and the Eighteenth Century*. Vol. 145. Oxford: The Voltaire Foundation, 1976. Print.

Rummel, Erika. *Colloqui di Erasmo da Rotterdam*. Milan: JACA, 1998. Print.

– *The Confessionalization of Humanism in Reformation Germany*. Oxford: Oxford UP, 2000. Print.

– *Erasmus*. New York: Continuum, 2004. Print.

– *Erasmus and His Catholic Critics*. 2 vols. Nieuwkoop: De Graaf, 1989. Print.

Safranski, Rüdiger. *Martin Heidegger: Between Good and Evil*. Trans. E. Osers. Cambridge, MA: Harvard UP, 1999. Print. Trans. of *Ein Meister aus Deutschland*. Munich: C. Hanser, 1994.

Sartre, Jean-Paul. *Situations* II. Paris: Gallimard, 1948. Print.

Saupin, Guy, ed. *La Tolérance : Colloque international de Nantes*. Rennes: Presses Universitaires de Rennes, 1998. Print.

– "Le concept de tolérance aux Temps modernes." *La Tolérance*. Ed. Saupin. 11–18. Print.

Schalk, F. "Erasmus und die *Res Publica Literaria*." *Actes du congrès Érasme, Rotterdam, 27–29 octobre 1969*. Amsterdam: North Holland Publishing Company, 1971. 14–28. Print.

Scherer, Jacques. "'L'univers en raccourci': quelques ambitions du roman voltairien." *Studies on Voltaire and the Eighteenth Century, Vol. 179*. Genève: Institut et Musée Voltaire, 1979. 117–42. Print.

Seebohm, Frederic. *The Oxford Reformers. John Colet, Erasmus and Thomas More*. Longmans, Green, 1869. Print.

Shakespeare, William. *The Riverside Shakespeare*. Eds. Blakemore et al. Boston: Houghton Mifflin, 1974. Print.

Spitz, Lewis. *The Protestant Reformation 1517–1559*. Rptd. with additions and corrections. St Louis: Concordia, 2001. Print.

Staël, Mme de. *De L'Allemagne*. 2 vols. Paris: Hachette, 1958. Print.

– *De la Littérature*. Paris: Classiques Garnier, 1996. Print.

Thompson, Craig R. "Erasmus and Tudor England." *Actes du Congrès Érasme Rotterdam 1969*. Amsterdam: North Holland Press, 1971. Print.

– Foreword. *Desiderius Erasmus Concerning the Aim and Method of Education*. New York: Bureau of Publications, 1964. vii–xxvi. Print.

– *Ten Colloquies of Erasmus*. New York: The Liberal Arts Press, 1957. Print.

Tocqueville, Alexis de. *Democracy in America*. Trans. George Lawrence. Ed. J.P. Mayer. New York: Harper and Row Perennial, 1988. Print.

Tombs, Robert, and Isabelle. *That Sweet Enemy: Britain and France: The History of a Love-Hate Relationship*. New York: Vintage, 2006. Print.

Trevor-Roper, H.R. "The General Crisis of the Seventeenth Century." *Crisis in Europe*. Ed. Aston. 59–95. Print.

Venard, Marc. "La France avant l'édit de Nantes." *L'Acceptation de l'autre*. Ed. Jean Delumeau. 21–34. Print.

Vives, Jaime Vicens. "The Decline of Spain in the Seventeenth Century." *The Economic Decline of Empires*. Ed. Cipolla. 121–67. Print.

Voltaire. *Appel à toutes les nations de l'Europe*. OC. Vol. 24. Paris: Garnier, 1879. 191–221. Print.

– *Candide*. *OC*. Vol. 48. Ed. René Pomeau. Oxford: Voltaire Foundation, 1968. Print.

– *Dictionnaire de la pensée de Voltaire par lui-même*. Ed. André Versaille. Paris: Édition complexe, 1994. Print.

– *Letters on England*. Trans. Leonard Tancock. London: Penguin, 1980. Print.

– *Mélanges*. Ed. Jacques van den Heuvel. Paris: Gallimard, 1961. Print.

– *Œdipe*. *OC*. Vol. 1A. Ed. David Jory. Oxford: The Voltaire Foundation, 2001. 15–284. Print.

– *Philosophical Dictionary*. 2 vols. Trans. unnamed. London: W.W. Dugdale, 1847. Print.

– *Romans et contes*. Eds. Frédéric Deloffre and Jacques van den Heuvel. Paris: Gallimard, 1979. Print.

– *Studies on Voltaire and the Eighteenth Century*. Vol. 48. Geneva: Institut et Musée Voltaire, 1966. 297–341. Print.

– "Voltaire's War with England." *Studies on Voltaire and the Eighteenth Century*. Vol.179. Geneva: Institut et Musée Voltaire, 1979. 79–100. Print.

Weber, Max. *The Protestant Ethic and the Spirit of Capitalism*. Trans. Talcott Parsons. New York: Scribner's, 1958.

Weil, Simone. *La pesanteur et la grâce*. Paris: Plon, 1988. Print.

William I of Orange. *The Apologie of Prince William of Orange Against the Proclamation of the King of Spain*, ed. H. Wansink, Leiden: E.J. Brill, 1969. Print.

Wilson, Derek and Felipe Fernández-Armesto. *Reformations: A Radical Interpretation of Christianity and the World, 1500–2000*. New York: Scribner's, 1996. Print.

Wilson, Edmund. *Patriotic Gore*. New York: Norton, 1994. Print.

Yeats. W.B. *The Collected Poems of W.B. Yeats*. Ed. Richard J. Finneran. New York: Macmillan, 1983. Print.

Zarka, Yves Charles, et al., eds. *Les fondements philosophiques de la tolérance*. Vol. 1 (Études), vol. 2 (Textes et documents). Paris: PUF, 2002. Print.

Index